teach yourself ®

grandparenting
the grandparents'
association

The Grandparents'
Association

teach yourself

1938
2008

celebrate
with us

Launched in 1938, the **teach yourself** series
grew rapidly in response to the world's wartime
needs. Loved and trusted by over 50 million
readers, the series has continued to respond to
society's changing interests and passions and
now, 70 years on, includes over 500 titles,
from Arabic and Beekeeping to Yoga and Zulu.
What would you like to learn?

be where you want to be with **teach yourself**

30 Milton Park, Abingdon, Oxon
0) 1235 400454. Lines are open
sage answering service. Details
achyourself.co.uk

ustomer Services, PO Box 545,
1726. Fax: 1-614-755-5645.

ill Ryerson Ltd, 300 Water St,
000. Fax: 905 430 5020.

d learning – with more than 50
s includes over 500 titles in the fields of languages, crafts, hobbies, business, computing and education.

British Library Cataloguing in Publication Data: a catalogue record for this title is available from the British Library.

Library of Congress Catalog Card Number: on file.

First published in UK 2008 by Hodder Education, part of Hachette Live UK, 338 Euston Road, London, NW1 3BH.

First published in US 2008 by The McGraw-Hill Companies, Inc.

This edition published 2008.

The **teach yourself** name is a registered trade mark of Hodder Headline.

Typeset by Transet Limited, Coventry, England.
Printed in Great Britain for Hodder Education, an Hachette Livre UK Company, 338 Euston Road, London NW1 3BH, by Cox & Wyman Ltd, Reading, Berkshire.

The publisher has used its best endeavours to ensure that the URLs for external websites referred to in this book are correct and active at the time of going to press. However, the publisher and the author have no responsibility for the websites and can make no guarantee that a site will remain live or that the content will remain relevant, decent or appropriate.

Hachette Livre UK's policy is to use papers that are natural, renewable and recyclable products and made from wood grown in sustainable forests. The logging and manufacturing processes are expected to conform to the environmental regulations of the country of origin.

Impression number   10 9 8 7 6 5 4 3 2 1
Year   2012 2011 2010 2009 2008

contents

acknowledgements

The Grandparents' Association is a UK national registered charity working to improve the lives of children by working with and for all grandparents. All royalties from this book will be used to support the work of the Grandparents' Association.

We would like to thank all the people who have contributed to chapters in this book:

Julia Chesterman, Lynn Chesterman and Caroline Needham who all work for the Grandparents' Association have made large contributions to the book as a whole.

'Helping grandchildren to learn' has been contributed by Jenny Cobbley, Director of the Learning with Grandchildren Basic Skills project at NIACE.

'Communicating with grandchildren' has been contributed by I CAN Director of Communications, Anita Kerwin-Nye.

'Disability in the family' has been contributed by Paul Smith of the Spinal Cord Injuries Association.

'In times of trouble' has been contributed by Margaret Wilson, Chair of the Magistrates Association.

We would also like to thank the many professionals and families who have generously contributed their time and energy to discussing the content of this book with the authors.

There never was a better time to be a grandparent. We live in an era when older people stay healthier for longer. The fitness and stamina you need to cope with young children are more likely to be yours than they were your grandparents. My own grandparents were born in the late nineteenth century when the life expectancy for both men and women was in their forties: it must have given a strange perspective on life to see your earthly span running out so soon. In fact, my grandmother lived into her mid-eighties and my grandfather into his nineties. They defied the statistics but they ran true to form in that people expected to age early. From their fifties my grandmother was stooped with rheumatoid arthritis, and my grandfather with rheumatism. Sprightly they were not!

Today's grandparents are an altogether livelier bunch: out on the golf courses and tennis courts, bowling like demons or cruising at leisure to places where the sun warms old bones. They can still dig a sand castle, have a stab at beach cricket, climb Glastonbury Tor, dance the tango. More thoughtfully they can read out loud poems they have known since their childhood, and lead the singing of nursery rhymes that today's parents hardly know.

Older people have memories freighted with gold: of how it was in the olden days before iPods and mobile phones, before DVDs, even before television. I am old enough to remember a wartime childhood and found it strange to be part of a question set for my grandchildren's homework. It ran thus: 'Find out from an old relation what the war was like.' Memories poured out and the young people marvelled that bombs could fall from the skies over Britain and that food could actually have been rationed.

This strikes at the core of the grandparent relationship, knowing how very different someone's life can be from your own. Coming to understand how others feel is one of the marks of growing up. The gift of empathy makes for a sympathetic nature and a thoughtful citizen. Coming to understand other generations is a step even further into making sense of how life works.

A grandparent is, after all, a link in the human chain that reaches back through centuries. That link gives us our background, our heritage and, we now understand, our genes. My own grandfather's memories included hearing Gladstone give an election speech, and embraced the horrors of the trenches and the great depression; my own include the second world war, the disclosure of the holocaust, and the spirit of the '60s; my grandchildren's lives will encompass the struggle against global warming. They may know space travel and miracles of science we cannot even imagine. Thus are we all links in the chain of generations that goes on down the centuries.

It is against such a background that grandparents today often have a far more diverse and active role than they used to have. With the trend for more mothers going out to work, grandparents regularly do much of the country's child care, very often freely given. They can find themselves a part of step-families, involved in adoption or fostering schemes, called on to witness civil partnerships, or with families at long distances speaking different languages, grandchildren of different races and different religions. All this is a challenge our own grandparents never faced, and there is much to be learned.

But the current generation of grandparents relishes the prospect. Older people's lives are busier than ever; the serious among them may be attending the University of the Third Age, or the Open University. A number of others recently got together to create a pop group called The Zimmers; a dance group of pensioners meet regularly at Sadlers Wells. More seriously they make be busy in politics. There is a fine record of grandparents actively campaigning to protect the lives of their families. In Argentina the 'Grandmothers of the Disappeared' marched each week in the centre of Buenos Aires to draw attention to their missing grandchildren. More recently Grandmothers Against the War founded in America in 2003 held regular Wednesday peace vigils in New York. We no longer just sit in corners wrapped in shawls or slump in deckchairs on windy seaside promenades. We are up and about, and doing.

As the years go by there are more and more of us. By 2074 there could be over a million centenarians. When we reach seventy we could well have twenty years more lively living to do. With so much of life rolling out ahead of us, we can take an active and affectionate part in the lives of our children and theirs. And, who knows, even in the fullness of time great-grandchildren, too. This book is a timely godsend to us all.

Joan Bakewell CBE

01

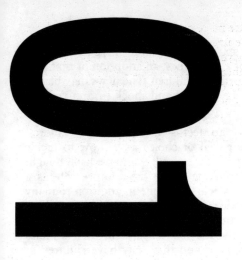

family life with a baby on the way

In this chapter you will learn:
- how to deal with your feelings as a new grandparent
- how to relate to your children as they become parents
- how to cooperate with the other grandparents
- how to cope with the feelings of your other children.

First reactions

Becoming a grandparent starts with the moment you receive the news from your child – of a pregnancy, an adoption or that they are to step-parent their partner's children. The news may be met with absolute joy, complete surprise and shock or a mixed bag of feelings.

There is no 'right' way to feel – as this book explores, grandparents have a great deal of choice as to how to tackle their new role. A number of readers will, perhaps, have bought this book as an aid to thinking about their future role as a grandparent. For many this role will come in addition to many others in their lives. Grandparents are likely to still be working and may have existing care commitments to older parents or younger children. For some the relationships in their families will encompass large age gaps and they may have children of their own little older than the new grandchild. Roles at work, at home and in the wider community may be little changed by becoming a grandparent, or for some becoming a grandparent may dramatically alter their priorities.

Most people find that becoming a grandparent and managing relationships within their family is a wonderful aspect of their lives. From the minute you hear that the baby is on the way you may be transported back to memory lane and become nostalgic for the time in your life when you were expecting a child. It may become difficult to resist the urge to give advice at this time, let your children make their own journey into parenthood and stay with that all the way through. If asked, offer to tell the new parents what you may have done in similar situations but remember that all pregnancies are different and your advice may not be a success in this case.

Estelle's story

Everyone says that people always remember where they were when they heard the news about the death of President Kennedy or John Lennon. For Estelle (and many other grandparents) she will always remember where she was – stuck in a traffic jam on the M6 when she heard she was to be a grandmother. Luckily she was not driving as her thoughts drifted as to whether it would be a boy or girl, what they would call it, what sort of pram would they want etc. and yet the event was months away!

Estelle also worried about what role she and her husband David would have as they are the dad's parents so they thought 'perhaps we won't be very involved'. David called their son immediately as his reaction was to ask their son if they were both happy with the somewhat unexpected news. When he assured him that they were then David could relax also. It seemed that the news had the same effect as when, long ago, they had discovered that they were to be parents – plans, hormones the lot.

Remember there will be other grandparents

In the midst of the euphoria it is easy to forget that the new child may come with a whole host of other grandparents. Apart from maternal and paternal grandparents there may be step-grandparents or great grandparents. This is not a competition to see who wins the most brownie points or spends the most money. If you have personal issues with one of the other grandparents (perhaps your ex wants to play a role or you have never got on with your child's in-laws) try to be sensible and think of the child first. They have a right to know their family background and have a relationship with other family members, so be sensible and do not allow personal feelings to colour your views unless you have some concerns about the welfare of the child.

Sometimes a new partnership will bring children into the family from previous relationships and this is covered in more detail in a Chapter 12. Becoming a grandparent may open up new areas of family communication about your adult child's own childhood and questions may be asked about decisions long forgotten.

Let the parents be the responsible adults

Babies and young children's needs are not primarily dependent on income or lifestyle, expecting a baby may trigger your son or daughter to make some changes – it is better to encourage them to talk about their plans rather than make assumptions about what they may be planning. Think long and hard about making any substantial offers of help – to provide childcare or large amounts of finance for example.

Instinctively new grandparents may wish to protect their children from the dramatic impact that parenthood will bring – the increased costs, the sleepless nights, the possible strain on their relationship and struggles to build a healthy work–life balance – with plenty of times for childcare. This is particularly true if you feel that your child is rather young to become a parent.

You will know that 'having it all' – the well paid job, an immaculate home, a contented baby and a great social life – is a huge challenge. Support your child in what is for most people their most life-changing adventure.

Annie's story

Annie has a close relationship with her mother which became closer while she was pregnant. She described being pregnant as being a special journey of discovery in preparation for her baby. She enjoyed talking to her mother as someone who had made that journey too – albeit a long time ago. What she most liked about her mother was that whilst she listened well she did not try to influence the choices her daughter was making.

Watch your behaviour

It is often the way you and other family members behave that most loudly communicates approval or disapproval of a younger generation's lifestyle. The parent who at every visit brings pregnancy vitamins, super foods, and also does all the laundry unasked is at risk of making themselves a martyr and making everyone else uncomfortable. Whereas the parent who visits, listens to their son or daughter and encourages them to enjoy planning for their baby is likely to be a welcome visitor. The role of grandparent can be fun and you can start to enjoy the thrill of imagining your new grandchild.

David and Rhiannon's story

David and Rhiannon had always been fiercely independent. Although they married at a young age they were lucky to have parents who supported but did not interfere. When they became grandparents they asked themselves if they would have welcomed any unsolicited 'advice' at various times in their lives and, on the whole, the answer was always 'no'. So they assumed that their equally independent sons and their partners would not welcome any interference in their lives and or advice on how they should raise their children. They recognized whenever they saw their children and grandchildren that they were doing a really good job on their own.

If you have had doubts or reservations about your son or daughter's choice of partner the expected birth of a grandchild is a good time to put these well behind you. Concentrate on finding opportunities to re-assess your relationship with their partner in their new role, especially since you now have a shared interest in the new baby and your relationship with your future grandchild.

The responsibilities of becoming a parent will be an exciting and happy time for most couples. But, for some, morning sickness and tiredness may put a strain on a relationship. If you are with your family and they start to bicker, give them some space – put in an offer to leave a little earlier than anticipated to enable them to have some privacy.

Your other children

At this time you may be aware that your other children are likely to be sensitive to their sibling becoming a parent. Take time to talk to them and beware of being seen to favour the expectant couple.

The MacDonald's story

In some families friendship between all those in the grandparent generation can help the children stay in touch with their extended family including aunts, uncles and cousins. The MacDonald family have a long tradition of the grandparents booking cheap holiday villas in Spain at off-peak rates for half-term week in February and October. The grandchildren look forward to seeing their cousins, uncles, aunts and grandparents on both sides of their family. Every year the family gather at Malaga airport and rent a minibus to drive to their destination. All the adults share the chores with their nephew, nieces and grandchildren and in the evenings the grandparent and parent generation take turns to babysit. The MacDonalds first started family holidays when their daughter-in-law, Amy, was pregnant with their first grandchild. They are very glad they also invited along Amy's parents and they have long believed that sharing holidays has been a good way to develop strong family ties.

Checklist

1 Treat all family members with respect and listen to their views.

2 Don't take sides in family disagreements – be prepared to alter your plans to ease tensions.

3 Help everyone in the family prepare for the new baby.

4 Plan family occasions well in advance and spend time together doing activities which the whole family can enjoy.

5 Take a moment to take stock of what becoming a grandparent means to you.

6 Remember being a grandparent is about a relationship not an indicator of your age.

7 Enjoy sharing the expectations of time with other grandparents and family members – do not compete.

8 Your son or daughter is the responsible adult who is becoming the new parent – support them and cheer them on.

9 Respect the decisions being made for your grandchild – do not try to alter the parents' views or plan to take over the role of parent.

02

support during pregnancy and adoption

As you may well remember yourself, every pregnancy is different. Some women glow with health and seem energized by their expectant bodies, others actually loose weight in the early stages of pregnancy having to contend with not just early morning but also 'rest-of-the-day' sickness. The expectant mother will first turn to the appropriate medical professionals to ensure that she and her baby are doing well and will have access to pre-natal care through the NHS in the UK or through her chosen health provider in the USA.

Your grandchild's father may be willing to attend pre-natal appointments, scans and classes. If this is not possible, because for instance they may have job commitments away from home, or the mother is single by choice, you may want to offer to help by going as a substitute. You may be excited to make such offers but do not be too disappointed if your offer is refused – some women may prefer to go along on their own.

Managing expectations

Seeing your child expecting a baby may well remind you of earlier days when you were expecting yourself and you may wish to share some of these memories. They will most likely not want to hear about this time in your life and don't tell any horror stories of past births. Rather look forward with them to the birth of your grandchild and treat it as their own unique and wonderful event. No one can imagine exactly what it will be like for them to bring a child into the world, for each of us it is a journey of discovery.

The expectant mother is more likely to talk to her friends, search the internet or read a book than ask for your advice. Most expectant mothers will attend classes and make their own birth plans after listening to the people who will be involved with them at the birth. Visiting websites, buying books and listening to the recent experience of friends will help them to choose a maternity hospital or help for a home birth. In understanding the choices she is making you may like to read some of the same literature to bring you up to date.

Frederico's Story

Frederico very much wanted to make a cradle for his first grandchild. His son Toni knew his wife Sophie was keen to use a cradle which had been in her family for a couple of generations. Toni told his dad about Sophie's family tradition and Frederico helped by collecting the cradle from Sophie's cousin in his van. Toni also asked for his dad's help in decorating the nursery and they spent many happy hours talking while they worked. Frederico was very proud of his son and Toni learnt a lot about family and fatherhood whilst they worked together.

Confidentiality

In the early stages of pregnancy the parents may well want to keep the pregnancy a secret and you may or may not be one of the few who knows their news. Families who have experienced a previous miscarriage may well feel nervous at this time – although you may share some of this anxiety try hard not to be overly concerned yourself. Remember most women who miscarry will go on to have healthy babies.

For some couples relationships can falter during pregnancy and the stress can resound around the extended family. If you know, for example, this was an unplanned pregnancy, ensure that you treat this as confidential information which was shared with you and avoid speculation about the future of their relationship.

Question:

My daughter is only sixteen and still at school and I am so shocked to find she is expecting a baby. I think the best thing I can do is look after my grandchild and let her get on with her life.

Answer:

Your daughter may well be delighted to have your support but it is important to respect that she is the parent and will have full responsibility for her baby. Many young parents rise to the responsibilities of parenthood and have no regrets at having children early in life. Your daughter will be able to take advantage of the fact that most colleges have crèches for students' children so, if she chooses, she will be able to continue her education whilst caring for her baby.

Buying for the baby

- You may wish to celebrate your forthcoming grandchild's birth by purchasing or knitting an entire wardrobe and buying all sorts of equipment.
- More than one new mother has felt upset that so little of her child's clothes were chosen by her.
- Avoid duplicating baby equipment by suggesting the parents let you know what they need and who else is buying.
- Many people are reluctant to have equipment delivered before the newborn is safely home – choose a 'buy now, deliver later' plan if this is available or postpone the purchase.
- Some babies are quite large when born and skip the newborn size entirely.
- An alternative to buying by yourself would be to put on offer a joint shopping spree with the parents that you would fund up to an agreed sum or to buy vouchers.
- Many expectant mothers will be saving money by economizing on their own clothes and small luxuries. A gift of luxurious lotions designed for the pregnant woman, a new maternity outfit or a bunch of flowers may be welcomed in the later stages of pregnancy.
- A less glamorous choice might be paying for some help in the home for a couple of weeks if the new parents would welcome this help before or after the baby is born.

Gwen's story

Gwen took to knitting big time when she was expecting her first grandchild. She felt as if this was her contribution to the whole waiting game and took pride in showing off all the delightful little outfits. When the baby was born he was a particularly hot baby and all the gorgeous clothes that other family and friends had bought when he was born were much more practical and sensible as they could be thrown in the washing machine. Consequently the little outfits were never worn.

The second little grandson was a summer baby so the clothes never got an airing. The knitting was very enjoyable for Gwen but not quite as useful as she had hoped. However, their mum kept them as sentimental items and Gwen was not upset because she had two wonderful grandsons. Next time round she went shopping for baby clothes instead!

Baby shower

A growing trend for expectant mums is the US-styled baby shower in which gifts are offered to the parents-to-be. If you think that this could be a fun thing to do for your family and friends you may want to discuss this with the expectant parents. You could throw this kind of a party once the news of the pregnancy is fully public and well before the baby's due date. A possible role for you could be to both host the party and informally be able to let guests know the contents of a baby wish list. As the parents themselves are the recipients of the baby gifts it is not appropriate for them to host it. If you know that money for baby equipment is very tight it could be that gift items from many people could be more acceptable than a lot of help from the grandparents. A number of specialist companies now advertise themed items such as 'nappy cakes' and party bags for guests but as a relatively new tradition grandparents may feel at liberty to improvise.

The wider family

- At the time you are expecting your grandchild you may want to think about the other grandparents and perhaps devote some time to thinking about future family relationships.
- For some families there may have been little contact in the past with your grandchild's other side of the family. Try to organize time to have a shared meal or social occasion with your in-laws in preparation for greater contact once the baby is born.
- Some joint planning of support for the family around the time of birth can save a scenario where grandparents feel slightly put out or displaced by each other.
- If you are in a situation where your immediate family has been affected by divorce or separation you may need to think about managing the situation with ex-partners in a way that enables you to relate comfortably with the new baby.
- If you have much younger children yourself you may want to think about working with your partner to identify time to spend supporting your older child as they become a parent.

Managing your own work–life balance

As a grandparent you may well know that babies have a largely unpredictable impact on their parents. The most career minded of people may, despite all plans to the contrary, decide to become a full-time, stay-at-home parent and others who had planned to be home-based pine for their working life to be resumed. All parents will want the best for their children and if you are asked to help it is good to have given your response some thought. The best advice would be not to hand in any notice to your own job or other commitments until well after the baby is born and the extent of your involvement has settled a bit. Some employers may be sympathetic to a request for additional leave, usually unpaid, around the time of the baby's arrival.

Avoid giving unwanted advice

- The way in which you are able to avoid too much advice-giving during pregnancy will bode well for the role of a grandparent.
- Many first-time mothers have the luxury of looking forward to a natural home birth with few complications. Other new mothers may opt for a caesarean birth in hospital on a date agreed with their obstetrician. You may be sceptical about home birth or disapprove of elective caesareans but now is not an appropriate time to get on your soap box but rather to take an interest in the expectant mother's own choice of birth plan.
- You will know that as the pregnancy develops plans may need to be amended. Every birth is different and no one can predict how short or long, easy or complicated your grandchild's birth will be.
- Facing the prospect of childbirth is a stage of life needing lots of support, reassurance and optimism; don't spoil this time with talk of anything else.
- This is a good time to pamper the expectant woman with your love, admiration, small gifts and emphasizing the qualities that she has which will make her a great mother. Praise the partner too for embarking on parenthood – telling them both you know they will be the best parents for their child. Also, remember to congratulate yourself on raising children who will become great parents.

Adoption

Grandparents may become a grandparent when their children choose to adopt a child or a sibling group. In the UK there are only a tiny number of babies available for adoption and the average age of an adopted child is four years old.

The adopting family

Adoptive parents will choose to adopt through an agency that will be staffed by specialist adoption social workers whose work will include training and assessing prospective parents and placement of children. The agency will want to be clear that the parents adopting will be comfortable taking on responsibility for a child who is not their biological child. Whilst they recognize infertility is commonly a reason for adoption they will want to ensure that parents, who may have been receiving infertility treatment, have come to terms with the loss of their prospect of a pregnancy and becoming a birth parent. The agencies now have inclusive policies that recognize that same sex couples and individual adopters are equally able to provide stable homes for children. The acceptance of grandparents and wider family when choosing to adopt will help support potential adopters through their training and assessment.

After initial group training the adoption social worker will make a detailed home study to assess the suitability of potential adopters for the task of parenting a young child. Their task will include assessing the wider context in which the family live and questions about, for example, their work–life balance and how this will adjust to taking on new parenting responsibilities.

The aim of the social workers will be to ensure the vulnerable children, whose birth parents are unable to care for them, are given a stable home and that the matching of children with adoptive parents is unlikely to break down. Whilst social workers will want to build a good working relationship with potential adopters they will also need to make thorough checks on all the people who will regularly be part of the child's life. The process may at times feel intrusive but asking probing questions about lifestyle and relationships is necessary to screen out those without the strengths to take on the challenge of adopting a child or children.

Once your family has been accepted as adopters they will wait for an appropriate match with a child needing adoption. The shortest wait is likely to be for a family group or a child with a disability. The early days of a new relationship with an adopted child or children are likely to present a significant challenge to the new parents. The family will have access to support and advice through the adoption agency but wider family and friends will also best help by holding back on judgements concerning the behaviour of the children and/or parenting advice.

The child's reactions

The Coram Family Adoption and Family Service in London have researched the impact on children of the adoption process. Children moving from fostering placements into adoption often experience a severe emotional reaction to being moved from their familiar surroundings to the home of their new parents. As many adopted children are beyond infancy their lives may have been exposed to a number of changes in those caring for them. They may have had an unhappy experience with their birth family and then been placed in a foster home for safety. It is likely that the child will have settled with their foster carer and may resent their more recent relocation to an adoptive home.

You will no doubt be sure that your family will provide their adopted children with all the love, care and security they will ever need. The early days of adoption may be quite difficult for all the parents who will want to settle their child into their new home, sensitive to the knowledge he or she may have experienced many changes in their short life. This can have the effect of causing the child to mistrust the adults in their lives.

It will take time, patience and understanding to enable the adopted child to feel safe and secure. Reactions to change may be puzzling to the wider family. Some children may react by being very 'adult' and appear to be mature beyond their chronological age – protecting themselves from let-down by appearing not to need a parent to comfort them or show physical affection. Some children will be much too friendly towards strangers and reject their new parents. The child may fear that all adults will be temporary visitors in their lives and fight against closeness for fear of being disappointed.

Another observed pattern in adopted children is regression into babyish behaviour, hiding their abilities and no longer willing to demonstrate the progress they had previously made. The behaviour of newly-adopted children can be very challenging and will need their new parents to react with patience, understanding and maturity. They will be helping their child to make a difficult journey from temporary care to a new and, for them, difficult adjustment to their new home. Learning to be part of a family will take time – and for some families a big part of the grandparents' support will be to emphasize to the child their parents are in charge. Children will be helped by an acknowledgement of the strong role their parents have – 'Let's ask your Mum/Dad first', 'Your Dad/Mum will want to know where you are'.

Whilst settling in children will need to first bond with their new parents, a consistent encouragement to show this by sitting with the parents, holding their hands and having the largest share of their attention will help. Initially an intense and sustained effort to build a secure basis for the future will require the parents to make looking after the child themselves a priority. It is likely to be a while before the child is ready or able to be looked after by other family members or cope with big family gatherings. There will be plenty of time later to absorb the child into the wider family.

Maddy and Kit's story

Maddy and Kit decided to become adoptive parents after they had been advised that their own chances of conceiving were not good following some unsuccessful attempts using In Vitro Fertilization (IVF) treatment. Maddy's mother Jill found it hard when friends enquired whether she was a grandmother yet. She had followed their wishes to keep their attempts to conceive confidential and realized this was the best course for everybody.

Jill was initially disappointed when Maddy told her that she and Kit would need to take several months before they could apply to be adoptive parents. She was also surprised to hear that they were looking to adopt a young child rather than a baby. After Maddy and Kit were accepted they adopted a little girl, Amy, who was four years old.

Jill wanted to rush around and organize a big family welcome party but Maddy and Kit were adamant this would not be wise. Jill would talk to Maddy every day on the phone and after a few weeks Amy began to respond to Maddy's patient and calm love and understanding. Jill was pleased that Maddy had a lot of support both from the adoption agency and her employer, who gave Maddy several months' adoption leave and the option to return part time when Amy started school.

Top tips for families adopting a child

- Accept that your adopted grandchild is likely to be a child rather than a small baby.
- Prepare for the adoption by sharing some of the information and advice offered to the adopting parents.
- Your grandchild will not settle with their new parents immediately – be guided by them as to how often to visit.
- Do not make judgements about the child based on their behaviour – they will have had an unsettled childhood to date and may not live up to your expectations.
- If you have concerns you may wish to contact the adoption agency for help.

Checklist

1 Let the parents decide when to 'go public' with news of the pregnancy and who will be told first.
2 Support the birth plans of the parents.
3 Offer a baby shower party for friends and family.
4 Offer your confidence and reassurance concerning parenting skills.
5 Hold back on any doubts or criticism.
6 Buy or borrow the same childcare manual the parents are reading.

03

grandparents and the newborn

Expectant parents are able to exercise more choice and control over how and where their baby will be born than was experienced by previous generations. Readers may themselves remember their own birth plans and attendance at antenatal classes as expectant parents. Many such classes now include an opportunity for a special session for grandparents which are an excellent opportunity to share in this learning. Many hospitals also offer the chance for a birth partner to be with the mother alongside the partner. In many cases this may be the grandparent. Your family will probably also be reading some books on baby and childcare, a tip to understanding their approach to parenting is to ask which one they are reading and to buy your own copy to study up.

In becoming a parent your adult child will be taking on what, for many, is a scary responsibility, and baby books, antenatal classes and advice from friends and family can never fully prepare the new parents. As a grandparent, you too may look back on your own first child for memories of the mixed emotions that can be triggered around this time.

Hannah and Martin's story

Hannah and Martin lived around the corner from their eldest daughter Emily and her husband Damien. They were thrilled when their granddaughter was born without any complications and returned home with her parents at 48 hours old. Hannah cooked extra portions of her daughter's favourite foods every day for a month. Each evening they would call round with piping hot food, lay it on the table for Emily and Damien, and then retreat home to eat their own dinner. Emily appreciated how having her mum care for her with her delicious food helped her to breastfeed and care for her baby without intruding on private time for her and Damien to bond with their baby.

Respect privacy

The dilemma for new grandparents is how they can balance their offers of help and support appropriately at this delicate time. Too much help could be interpreted as taking over and that the grandparent is lacking confidence in the new parents' ability to cope. However, a lack of help or interest, although triggered by a desire not to interfere, could be interpreted as a lack of loving care or interest. Many grandparents recognize this dilemma and if you have friends who are already grandparents they may be an important source of support for you – particularly if the new parents would prefer a lot of time on their own with their new baby. Many paediatricians and psychologists recognize the importance for some parents to cocoon themselves with their newborn as a very helpful start to a child's life. As a grandparent you must remember, this is just the beginning of a long relationship with a younger generation – a few days extra to wait will not result in long-term exclusion.

Carol's story

Carol had planned with her husband that his parents would visit from the USA soon after her first son was born. Her in-laws holiday trip included a bed and breakfast holiday and sightseeing for all of them. As a first-time mother she had not understood how difficult it would be to look after a baby in holiday accommodation. Her son had been overdue and was exceptionally thin, tall and hungry but otherwise healthy and though she was struggling she was determined to breastfeed. Carol's mother-in-law was extremely worried over her thin grandson and begged to be allowed to bottle feed him as she had bottle fed her children. Carol's father-in-law was fascinated by breastfeeding which he had not observed before and wanted to watch, but she found his close-range observation unsettling and needed more privacy. Tensions escalated to high levels of conflict and anxiety which exacerbated Carol's problems with producing sufficient milk. One of Carol's close friends immediately observed her difficulties and she invited everyone to her house for dinner. During the visit she took Carol's in-laws aside and made the case for respecting her decisions and her need for privacy.

The maternal grandparents

New mothers may show a preference for involving their own parents in care of their baby at an earlier stage than the father's parents. It is more common for example for women to ask their mothers to be present at the birth than the mother of the baby's father. The wise paternal grandparent will not take such a choice in a way that hinders future relationships. It is just natural that a first-time mother feels more comfortable sharing the intimacy of childbirth with her own mother.

Question:

I don't know my daughter-in-law very well and I am afraid she will not want me to be involved with the baby – what can I do?

Answer:

Write and tell her how happy you are that she is expecting your grandchild – tell her how confident you are she will be a good mother and that you will be guided by her as to what help she would like.

Birthing options

Hospital birth

- It's important to remember that your child's experience of hospital and medical care may be very different to yours.
- Recently many hospitals have worked hard to improve their maternity services and respond positively to parental choices.
- Over time professional practice around supporting new parents has changed – for example an uncomplicated birth of a full-term baby may involve less than 24 hours in a maternity hospital.
- Some mothers will have access to purpose designed maternity suites which may include options such as the possibility of an active birth including pools suitable for water births and all hospitals will encourage active involvement of a birth partner.

The grandparents may find that in the haste and panic of going into labour the phone calls on progress were not made. Babies seldom arrive according to plan and when swept up in the moment no new parent deserves complaints about who got told what when! Whenever the news reaches you let it be welcome – if plans changed which resulted in relatives finding out a few hours later than expected then so be it. The news is exciting and grandparents may want to phone all the family – ask the new parents if they would prefer to do this themselves. Similarly, sensitivity is needed around circulating birth announcement cards and photographs.

Home birth

- Home births are experiencing a growing popularity and for some mothers the prospect of giving birth at home is an attractive option.
- Grandparents can be assured that planned home births are associated with positive outcomes for both baby and mother.
- Some parents wanting to ensure continuity of care throughout pregnancy and childbirth may choose to use the service of an independent midwife who may also be able to offer access to a specialist birthing centre.
- Research has shown that for the majority of mothers with uncomplicated pregnancies, babies thrive when delivered by a familiar midwife at home.
- Some pregnancies associated with high-risk birth (e.g. multiple births) may be considered unsuitable for a home birth and all midwives will have the knowledge of and access to hospital resources in the rare event of a transfer to hospital becoming necessary.

Prematurity

- A premature baby is defined as being born before 37 weeks gestation.
- If your grandchild is born early the good news is that over time survival rates have improved dramatically.
- At such times your anxiety will be focused on the survival of the baby in your family. Be strong for your adult child, listen and nurture them through their anxiety and keep the outside world at bay whilst they spend their hours at the hospital. In their shock and anxiety parent them by emphasizing their baby needs them to be healthy and that requires some nourishment and rest if they can manage it.
- Phone your friends and other family members for your own support. If you need to find out more about any specific problems or conditions use one of the excellent websites or helplines at the back of this book to find out more.

Supporting the new parents

A grandparent laying the basis for a supportive role in their grandchild's life will first and foremost acknowledge that all key decisions will be taken by the parents and whatever their own views they will recognize that the new parents are primarily responsible for their child. Everyday decisions for newborns – breast or bottle feeding, using or not using a dummy, or sleeping in bed with parents are just a few of the topics on which feelings may run high. The primary needs of newborns are for milk, cuddles, warmth and to be kept clean and safe. Being available 24 hours a day to provide care for a newborn is likely to be all absorbing for new parents, other relationships to work, friends and family and the wider world will temporarily recede.

- You can help by looking after the parents' own needs, providing encouragement, appetizing food, help with chores and facilitating time to sleep and have a bath or shower.
- Tiredness, hormones and unfamiliar responsibilities may cause some irritability and tension between you and your child. This is an appropriate time for praise and empathy – tell your family how wonderful they are and how much you admire them.
- If the parents refuse help admire their independence – you may put help on offer but it is up to them whether to accept it.
- New parents may prefer to be alone with their baby and not to share the early days with anyone but their partner.

Positive reinforcement

- Looking after new parents who are caring for their baby is a challenge but if parents accept practical help and emotional support such help can be an enormous boost to their ability to cope.
- Be positive and praise their good qualities, hold back on criticism.
- Tell them that they are doing well and that they are caring, loving parents.
- Observe that their baby is content/well nourished/lively/intelligent/loved/cared for and a lucky baby to have been born into a great home.
- Reassure them that they have the right priorities (e.g. babies needs over housework) and allow them to choose their support from family.

Maria's story

Maria's children grew up in terry-towelling nappies. When changing her grandson she was confronted by the latest in disposable ones that wrapped themselves around the baby and stuck to everything it shouldn't. Time for a lesson. Her husband succeeded much better than she did at first. Her nappy attempts plunged to the baby's ankles as soon as she picked him up and both grandparents managed to put at least one on back to front!

Maria also had to be educated with the bottles. Milk arrived in ready-mixed cartons; there was an electric sterilizer that steamed everything clean (what happened to leaving them overnight in a container with tablets and a pail of nappies in the bathroom?) and the teats on the bottles had a little hole that had to go the right way round. Maria felt that babies had been spit roasted over the years! Were they to go on their back, side or front? How on earth was she meant to set up a travel cot that became so deep that she struggled to put the baby down or pick him up again without dropping him or doing irreparable damage to her back?

The straps on the pram (not the good old carriage pram) and the car seats all needed a degree in applied science to sort out and, in an effort to be so super cool Maria had to ask another family in the car park how to open up the pushchair! She and her husband were so worried about the baby and getting the straps right that they emerged from their first shopping trip with the baby to find that the week's shopping had been left in the trolley in the car park! Thankfully the supermarket had taken care of it for them and delivered it later that day.

A helping hand

This is the time to offer help – see checklist below. Rather than do all these tasks yourself you may want to help organize a rota including other family and friends who can help out. If there are other young children in the family help them feel included by adding their names as helpers with adult supervision – this will often work well with an aunt, uncle, cousin or family friend.

* Cleaning
* Laundry
* Shopping
* Cooking

- Looking after pets
- Watering plants/gardening
- Watching over baby while parents sleep or bathe
- Acknowledging gifts/phone calls
- Sorting gifts of baby clothes into sizes and labelling for future use
- Changing nappies
- Organizing repairs/finishing DIY tasks
- Driving the new mother to appointments
- Assisting with arrangements for naming ceremonies
- Researching (but not choosing) childcare options
- Negotiating with friends and family who visits and when
- Finance (see Chapter 06 for details)
- Making coffee/tea for visitors
- Screening phone calls and visitors.

Question:

My son is expecting us to move closer to the family so that we can help more when the baby is born – it is flattering to be asked but we would miss our friends and interests in our home town. Should we move?

Answer:

Explain to your son that you enjoy your independence and will stay where you are. You may wish to put on offer staying with or near them to help from time to time whilst maintaining your current home.

Naming the baby

Many people faced with naming a child are amazed at the complexity of making their decisions. Their first choice of name may meet with opposition from a partner or members of their family. Some cultures and some families may have naming traditions to be followed or broken with and grandparents may have an important role in supporting the choices their children have made. Children with dual heritage may need names to reflect both cultures and may need to negotiate whether the child will be formally named within either culture, neither or both.

Celebrities have recently set trends for naming their children after the place of conception or a fruit. Such fashions for names change over time and grandparents may be surprised at the choice of names for the newborn. Whatever the name the baby will come to respond to the sound of their name and whatever their name they may or may not be teased in the playground. If the baby is named after a family member or friend this is a very special compliment. Babies and small children often have their names shortened or acquire nicknames unrelated to their given name. A good start is to stick with the diminutive chosen by the parent(s).

Behaviour and discipline

Every generation is influenced by a range of influential people who promote certain approaches to managing the behaviour of babies and children. As a new parent with the prospect of responsibility for raising a child it can seem like an open season for information and advice-giving from all quarters – health professionals, nurses, family, friends, books, television programmes, websites and even strangers in the supermarket offer 'friendly' advice. The new parent may find it hard to make sense of their role in ensuring their child is bought up well.

New babies will naturally exhibit a range of different behaviours and watching their own child's behaviour is the single most useful guide to the parental/caring response needed. The desire to parent well can be a great source of anxiety for your adult child and so positive encouragement can help parents relax and enjoy their new role. Love them and their growing children and help them to laugh with you and support their parenting.

Rosie's story

When Rosie had her grandchildren to stay she would start each visit by playing a game called 'In Grandma's House'. In the game she would get her grandchildren to remember the things she liked to happen at her house. At the end of the game she would give each of them a big hug and tell them how proud she was they had remembered – hanging up their coats, closing the garden gate, washing hands before meals and other good things they would do when with her. She would gently remind them of anything else she wanted them to remember.

The game was such a success that her daughter Amanda adapted it to a game called 'When I'm at home' which she played with her children when they came back from staying with Grandma Rosie.

Additional approaches

- Children copy those they see around them and grandparents can show children how to act by example – holding hands while walking in a busy street and being allowed to run ahead a little way in the park for example.
- The parents will be teaching their children to behave in a good way and you can help encourage them while they are with you.
- If your grandchild is not behaving as you want make sure your response is kind and firm. Tell your grandchild what behaviour you are looking for.
- If you lose your temper make sure to control your response to your grandchild rather than get angry and shout or physically hurt your grandchild. If you are worried you are about to lose your temper place your grandchild in a safe place (e.g. their cot) and go and get a quick break to cool down.
- Punishment that includes a smack can cause your grandchild to be hurt, upset and unable to remember why they were smacked.
- Children will want to know why they have to behave in a certain way and a good explanation ('I want to make sure you are safe and close by while I walk down the street.') will help children behave as you want them to.

Richard's story

When Richard looked after the grandchildren his wife had to remind him not to swear when he wrestled with the straps and to get used to the fact that his three-year-old granddaughter could work the DVD better than he could!

Question:

My grandchild is very badly behaved and just helps himself to food and borrows my things without asking, what can I do?

Answer:

Your grandchild's behaviour may be showing that he feels right at home in your house and is behaving accordingly. Describe to him the arrangements in your home – ask him to check with you before he goes to the refrigerator or uses any of your things. As his behaviour may be fine at his home explain that things are different in your house.

Please and Thank you

Many grandparents place much emphasis on children remembering to say 'please' and 'thank you' and also writing formal thank-you letters for presents at birthdays and other family occasions. It's lovely to have letters from children but is it worth risking falling out with your family if they do not put the thanks in writing? Lead by example by writing them notes of thanks for their presents to you. Help the parents by offering to sit down to help the children write thank-you notes for their gifts from other friends and relatives after a birthday or Christmas.

Joy's story

When Ella was four she stayed with her grandmother Joy and often forgot to say 'please' when she wanted a drink or snack. Joy decided to use the same prompt as she had with her own children, 'Ella what's the magic word?' she asked. 'Abracadabra' said Ella. 'Do you think I'm a witch?' said Joy, and Ella laughed and laughed and has called Joy Granny Witch ever since.

Crying babies

All babies cry as their way of telling the people who care for them they need something; they may need food, to have a nappy changed, or to be held and comforted. A loving cuddle and talking quietly to a baby is the most natural way for families to look after their babies. Babies need people near them and for people to talk to them in order to be able to learn how to communicate. New parents may worry that their baby is disturbing others – you can help by reassuring the parents how healthy their baby is and how he/she will grow up to be a great talker! Babies and parents are much more likely to relax when their ordinary behaviour is accepted and appreciated.

At an early life stage it is important to recognize that good research has demonstrated that babies are not capable of manipulation or being a 'good' or 'bad' baby. Unconditional love and acceptance will help everyone to relax. The parents may feel very tired and think they are unable to go out due to their crying baby. Babies will often go to sleep easily with their grandparents if they can remain calm and this helps everyone to enjoy life. Grandparents can offer to babysit or take the baby out to give Mum and Dad a break.

Angie's story

Angie went with her son to visit the home of her newborn grandson. She was delighted that her son-in-law, Peter, put the baby to bed whilst she chatted to her daughter Cheryl. The family sat talking amicably until the baby started crying, at which point Peter rushed to his son's cot and picked him up for a cuddle. Angie was outraged that her grandson was being spoilt and would be a completely undisciplined child. She told her daughter that she should not let her husband cuddle the baby so easily but far from agreeing with her mother Cheryl said that she and Peter would decide how to bring up the baby. Angie immediately asked her son to take her home as it was 'obvious she was not welcome'.

When Angie got home she realized she had got it wrong. She phoned the next day to tell Cheryl what a wonderful dad Peter was turning out to be. She told her daughter she had realized that it was hard for her to see Peter help so much when she had coped alone as a single parent.

Soon after Angie had some counselling and found it helped her deal with some problems in her past and improve her relationship with her daughter.

Babysitting

Copy their home routine

- If you are looking after your grandchildren share with their parents the regular features of their day.
- Small children benefit from living to a regular rhythm of waking and sleeping, eating, playing and quiet down time.
- Most children become a bit scratchy and irritable when hungry or tired – calmly giving them food or the opportunity for a cuddle and a nap will often be the simplest remedy.

Babyproof your home

- Children are naturally curious and babies will put everything in their mouth to explore the texture. Crawling babies will stick their fingers in anything and toddlers relish the excitement of being in a new environment.
- Help everyone relax by moving precious and fragile objects out of reach, if a chair has been newly upholstered it can

easily be protected from sticky fingers and other accidents by covering it up with a sheet or throw.

- If a small child is reluctant to relinquish something important to you such as the house keys, try distracting them with a new activity – playing with something else or looking out of the window.

- Cover up plugs with special covers available from children's shops or hardware stores.

For more details on child-proofing see Chapter 04.

Top tips

- Accept that the parents will be responsible for setting boundaries for their children and making decisions about discipline.

- Praise is a great motivator – use it frequently to reward good behaviour.

- Describe the behaviour you would like from your grandchild and express your delight at his/her cooperation.

- Give hungry children food and tired children sleep rather than argue with them.

- Let your grandchildren enjoy their time with you and never criticize the way they are being bought up by their parents.

Children are individuals

- Take time to observe your grandchildren and their behaviour with their parents and other adults.

- Younger children may have forgotten any requests made to them earlier in the day. Remind children gently and repeat your requests rather than scolding them.

- Some children are anxious to please and likely to go along with anything you suggest whilst others will want to challenge your instructions and find out what will happen if they disobey.

- Children respond well to being liked and loved for their unique personalities and praised for their cooperation.

- It is not helpful to compare a child with other members of the family or describe them as naughty or 'bad' children.

- It is more helpful to describe the behaviour you like and ask for their help, making clear as to how you would like them to behave when they are with you.

- Praise is a very good way of raising healthy, happy children. When children have done a good job make sure they know you are pleased with them.

Difficult times

- Children benefit from their grandparents understanding that they will not always be feeling happy and bright.
- A child who is looking sad probably is feeling down and may welcome some space as well as some time to talk about what is happening in their life.
- Children need reassurance that their feelings are noticed and if their feelings are overwhelming they may produce attention-grabbing behaviour.
- It's important not to reward negative behaviour, rather tell your grandchild you are displeased by the behaviour and later tell your grandchild you love them and wonder if perhaps they are having a bad day and if they would like to talk about it.
- If you think you know what might be upsetting them you might check out your assumptions and let your grandchild know that you understand if, for example, their sister is ill and they are worried. It can be very reassuring for children to be able to know that adults are also upset – even very young children will know when the grown-ups around them are anxious.

Checklist

1 Most adults have a great capacity for playing and creating fun. As a grandparent you can afford to be relaxed with your grandchildren, knowing that you are in a supporting role in their childhood – able to applaud their achievements and congratulate their parents.

2 Your most important contribution is to love and nurture the parent generation knowing as you do what a difficult task parenting can be.

3 You can help parents by giving them positive feedback on the way their children behave and reassurance that their child is growing up well.

4 Enabling parents to get a break while you to look after their precious child will help them cope with the hard job of raising their child.

04

grandparents and childcare

In this chapter you will learn:
- how to child-proof your home for babysitting
- why you need to balance your work and childcare responsibilities
- how to use local resources like baby and toddler groups.

In recent years there has been a rapid rise in the number of grandparents who regularly provide childcare for their grandchildren. This is due to more mothers returning to work and the lack of affordable childcare places which means that many families rely on the goodwill and support of grandparents to look after the grandchildren. In 2007 a survey commissioned by the Skipton Building Society estimated that grandparents providing childcare for their grandchildren saved their families £7 billion a year in childcare costs in the UK.

Offering to help

Increasingly pregnant women are turning to their mothers and/or mothers-in-law to assist them with childcare to cover the hours when they return to work.

There is no right answer as to whether you should agree to do this. If you are thinking of offering to help you may want to have a quick reality check as to how manageable the workload of looking after a baby will be.

It may be that you are reluctant to give up your job and would have some difficulty returning to employment when your grandchild is older. You may have several adult children and feel you are unable to care for a potentially large number of grandchildren over a prolonged length of time. Perhaps you would like some one-on-one time caring for a grandchild but not on a five-days-a-week basis? Quite possibly you may be over the moon at the prospect of full-time grandparenthood and frustrated by any thoughts otherwise.

Flexible working

Working parents are now able to request part-time work; in some families a rota of people in an extended family network regularly care for small children. This can include grandparents and parents all negotiating some flexibility in their work to enable them to all combine some paid work with childcare. Some day-care facilities and some childminders now provide part-time placements which can cover part of the working week whilst families cover the rest of the time.

Freelance work can be particularly difficult as it may be harder than new parents think to work at home with a small baby.

They may need to find this out for themselves before accepting help.

Although grandparents who still work themselves are less likely to be able to help look after their grandchildren, recent figures show that nearly one-fifth of employed grandparents are providing childcare for their grandchildren three or more times a week. In addition, many working grandparents contribute financially to the childcare costs for their grandchildren.

For many grandparents it can sometimes seem that their dream of a peaceful retirement and having the time to get around to doing all those things they had been looking forward to may have to be put on hold. In some families caring for the youngest generation is shared by the great-grandparents as well, particularly when the grandparents are still working.

Currently grandparents and other relatives who provide childcare for their grandchildren or young relatives are classed as 'informal' childcare.

Hannah's story

I care for my granddaughter from 6.30 a.m. until 6.00 p.m. because the parents commute to London. It's a 12-hour day. It's difficult in wet or cold weather because my granddaughter, who is three, still wants a lot of physical attention. Grandparents are physically different from mums, some grandmas say, 'I could do it one day but not all week'. Most days we read each other stories to try to settle her for a sleep for an hour or two. Three mornings each week she goes to playschool. As a result of the childcare commitments I have also moved to be nearer my family but I haven't had time to make friends here much...

Susan's story

Sometimes you need to be around older people otherwise you can get bogged down with children and grandchildren. You need a life of your own; you need a balance. I love looking after my grandchildren but I need one or two days (in the week) to do what I want to do, whether it be my shopping, cleaning, dancing or seeing my friends for coffee or lunch. If I had the grandchildren everyday it would become too much, it wouldn't be just a happy, enjoyable thing then.

Childproofing your home

Grandparents who regularly look after their grandchildren may want to consider taking steps to childproof their homes. Below are some ideas to help keep the children safe when they visit. As you will remember from when your own children were young, small children should never be left unsupervised how ever much you have done to childproof your home.

Cabinets

Kitchen and bathroom cabinets often contain things that are unsafe for children such as cleaning materials and medicines. Most DIY stores and specialist children's stores sell a selection of safety cabinet locks which, if properly installed, will allow for easy access by adults but will keep little hands from prising the cabinets open.

However, no safety lock can completely guarantee that a child won't be able to get into a cabinet. Store any hazardous materials or other items that pose a risk in a high cabinet with a lock that is well out of the reach of small children.

Stairways

When young children are in the house it's a good idea to install safety gates at both the top and bottom of all stairways. However, even the best safety gates cannot keep children safe around stairs if they are not used regularly and it is a good idea to try to get into the habit of keeping the gates closed even when the grandchildren aren't around.

Beware of children trying to climb over gates as they get older – discuss with your family when it is safer to remove them.

Toys

Every year toys that would fail British safety standards are sold illegally at knock-down prices at car boot sales and markets. Recent examples in the UK have included teddy bears with loosely fixed eyes on sharp metal sticks and toy cars that have been painted with lead paint. Even well-known manufacturers have had cause to recall some items recently because of safety concerns. Watch out for recall notices in stores where you shop.

Ensure your grandchild is safe by buying from reputable shops or borrowing toys from your local toy library.

Clothes

Some grandparents may enjoy knitting or sewing clothes for their grandchildren. If so, do remember small buttons or ties will pose a danger for babies or toddlers.

Any sewing or knitting equipment box needs putting well out of reach of children and sewing machines need to be kept covered up when children are visiting.

Outdoor safety

Gardens and garages

When childproofing your home it is also important to consider the outdoor areas that your grandchild(ren) may have access to:

- Most garden sheds and garages store a number of hazardous things such as tins of paint/oil and power tools. It is essential to make sure that young children cannot access these areas which should be kept locked at all times when they are around.
- Garden ponds should not be accessible to young children and if possible should be fenced off, covered or even filled in. No child should be left alone near water as drowning accidents can happen very quickly, even with a shallow amount of water.

Road safety

Children under three years old will need to use an appropriate child restraint when being transported in either the front or rear of a vehicle. They cannot be carried in a car that does not have seat belts because it will not be possible to fit a child restraint in such vehicles. Children between three and 12 also need an appropriate child restraint when riding in the front or back seat of a vehicle. In the UK it is the driver's responsibility to ensure that children under 14 years old use an appropriate child restraint or wear their seat belt.

If you regularly use your car to transport your grandchildren you may find it easier to purchase your own seat for your car as many models take time and patience to transfer from one car to another.

Baby and toddler groups

For many grandparents who look after young children during the day, there is often a feeling of isolation. You may feel as if you cannot see your friends as much if you always have the grandchildren in tow.

The Grandparents' Association has set up a number of grandparent and toddler groups in some areas of England, which give grandparents with childcare responsibilities a chance to meet up with others in a similar situation and make new friends. If you would like to start a facility in your area contact your national grandparenting organization for help.

In areas where there is no grandparent and toddler group available the Pre School Learning Alliance (UK) or YMCA (USA) may well have baby and toddler groups that will welcome grandparents and their grandchildren. They may even have other grandparents who regularly attend the group. (See Taking it further for more details.)

Part-time care

If you are finding looking after your grandchildren all the time is a daunting prospect it's a good idea to sit down with their parents and look creatively at how your family could work with you to reduce the pressures of your role.

- In some families this can be achieved by one or both parents reducing their hours to spend more time with their children.
- Another option is to see if the other grandparents would like to share with the childcare on a regular basis.

You might also like to explore whether a local nursery or childminder has some availability of a place for your grandchild full or part time. This would enable you to combine childcare with some rest and relaxation and a chance to catch up with friends and hobbies.

Question:

I love my grandson James very much but I don't want to look after him while his parents work as his parents expect me to. How can I tell them?

Answer:

Be clear that you are not available to look after James during working hours. It is up to his parents to make arrangements for him and they need to know as soon as possible that you are not available. You do not need to give reasons just state clearly that you love them all and if you feel you want to put on offer other help, for example helping with the cost or some evening babysitting.

Balancing care for all your grandchildren

As time goes by you may find yourself with several sets of grandchildren with an expectation that you will find some time and energy to look after all of them. It is well worth ensuring that all of your family feel equally valued and that your attention is shared.

Checklist

1 Talk through with the parents all aspects of any arrangements to provide regular childcare. Decide with them what hours will be involved and where care will take place.

2 Make arrangements to cover what will happen if you need a break or become ill. Work out with the parents a back-up care plan.

3 If your grandchild will be a frequent visitor keep duplicate sets of equipment and a box of favourite toys at your house. Check with parents on preferences relating to TV viewing, sweets and nap times etc.

4 If you are taking on regular childcare at your grandchild's home make clear whether your offer will include assisting with any household chores such as washing, cleaning and/or caring for pets.

5 Make sure that you have all the contact telephone numbers for parents including where they will be – they may have mobiles switched off at meetings or conferences.

6 Join in local child focused activities such as baby and toddler groups to help you and your grandchildren make friends and learn new games.

7 Make some time to spend having fun with the parents.

8 Remember to leave some time for yourself as well, you deserve to have some leisure time to fulfil your chosen pursuits.

05

feeding your grandchild

In this chapter you will learn:
- the grandparents' role when the mother is breastfeeding
- when babies are ready to be weaned
- what to feed toddlers
- how to help overweight children and children with eating disorders.

Generations of children growing up in the same family will experience very different attitudes to food and nutrition reflecting the prevailing availability of food, income, advice from health visitors and the media. As we write, early in the twenty-first century, families are berated by the media for raising sedentary, overweight children or teenagers with serious eating disorders.

In the UK and USA many news organizations thrive on sensationalizing crimes against children with the consequence that fewer children walk to school or play outside their homes to get enough exercise.

The celebrity and fashion industry is increasingly obsessed by the slightest variation in the weight of models and celebrities. The journalists writing about them are seldom qualified to distinguish between those who are slim and healthy and those with a serious eating disorder. Sadly, a growing number of children are very concerned about their weight and may develop a difficult relationship with the food that they eat.

Different family attitudes to appropriate food and snacks for children and eating meals together, whether or not in front of the TV, can become the basis of family feuds between adults and very confused children. A growing number of people are choosing to become vegetarian or vegan and in dual heritage families religious traditions in both families will dictate the menu on days of significance in the religious calendar.

Additional factors that worry some parents are concerns about farming methods, the content of manufactured food and the energy consumed in getting food to the table. Fears about young children being exposed to too much salt or eating peanuts are based on the reality that such foods are potentially harmful and in some tragic cases fatal to young children. Children with certain medical conditions such as asthma or diabetes will receive dietary advice from the medical personnel they consult which needs to be shared with grandparents. Young children with heart conditions may also have diets that could include foods with a high fat content. The advice on diet for young children with a specific condition can be very different to that for an older adult with the same or similar condition.

Babies

- The decision to breastfeed or bottle feed a newborn is personal to the mother. The likelihood is that she will be strongly advised and encouraged to breastfeed. The choice to breastfeed will be most easily made by those mothers who feel confident and comfortable to nurse their babies.
- If the mother is breastfeeding ensure that she has a comfortable place to breastfeed and be supportive if she prefers to breastfeed in private or if she is happy to breastfeed in public.
- If mothers choose to bottle feed their babies they will, perhaps, have experienced some pressure to try to breastfeed and their use of formula may have been frowned on.
- Try not to comment on the mother's choice. Whatever choice is made the new baby will initially feel most comfortable being cuddled whilst feeding, secure in the arms of their family.
- A grandparent may wish to feed their grandchild. If the baby is being breastfed this may be organized once breastfeeding is well established if the mother is happy to express their milk in advance – but some mothers hate the task of milking themselves.
- Mothers may be more willing to allow grandparents to give a formula feed. How often and how much a baby is fed should always be guided by the mother's wishes.
- If a baby is being breastfed it is important not to supplement with formula unless this has been medically advised.
- When using formula or breast milk that has been expressed make sure to immediately throw away any that is not finished. Babies are vulnerable to infection and throwing away the unfinished milk will ensure no one mistakenly gives the baby milk that has been sitting around for a while and may be unsafe.

Weaning

Over time advice on how soon to introduce some solid food has changed. Currently the medical profession prefer that parents delay the introduction of solid food until the baby reaches six months old. Whilst at this stage weaning foods can be added, cow's milk should not be drunk until the baby reaches 12 months. Therefore, breast milk or formula will still be an important part of their diet.

- The decision as to when to wean is always one that the parents need to consider carefully and may be influenced by a number of factors including weight gain, frequency of feeding, behaviour of the baby and professional advice.
- The time when babies are coping with their first solid foods may be a time when extra help from a grandparent is most welcome – particularly if there are twins in the family.
- Babies can be at risk of choking if left alone with their food.

Baby foods

- Some grandparents may be horrified at the cost of a tiny jar of baby food particularly if it is organic.
- Busy parents will often choose to use prepared baby foods that come from a particular range and will, perhaps, provide such food for visits or babysitting.
- Of course, many others will choose to cook and prepare food themselves and include ripe bananas or avocados on the menu.
- Eggs, cow's milk and honey can cause digestive problems in babies and should not be used until they have a more mature digestion.

It is wise to work closely with parents to develop the baby's diet as he/she grows older. If you are cooking a family meal make sure to omit any salt in vegetables such as potatoes if they are likely to be mashed up for the baby. Never be tempted to substitute baby foods with regular foods such as instant porridge as the regular products are very likely to contain salt and be too rough for the baby's developing digestive system.

Toddlers

- As children grow older their tastes will be guided by their family and increasingly by those who regularly look after them in their homes or a day-care setting.
- Most children over one year old will need to drink milk. If you usually have skimmed or semi-skimmed milk you could make sure that full-fat milk is available for your grandchild.
- Some children may not tolerate dairy products in which case soya milk is usually the substitute chosen. Nowadays this is stocked in most supermarkets and health food stores.
- Check with parents whether the children have any allergies. Do not try any new foods that may cause allergic reactions, e.g. peanuts.

- When visiting, all children need a balanced intake from different food groups; do not worry if a child picks and chooses at one meal and leaves food uneaten. Insisting that everything on the plate is finished may mean the child overrides the feeling they are full and this may contribute to them gaining too much weight when they are older.

- Many grandparents may include foods with high fibre content in their own diet – for example wholewheat cereals, wholewheat pasta and brown rice. These foods are hard to digest for children and are not recommended for children under five.

- Many families will try to keep their children away from sweets, ice creams and crisps for as long as possible. As a grandparent it is best not to introduce your grandchild to such foods. When your family visit remember to stock up with a large fruit bowl rather than chocolates and crisps – once they have left the remains will be better for you too! If you do want to offer some special treats double check with the parents first.

- Most children will enjoy helping in preparing food and finding out about their food. It can be very exciting for city children without gardens to help pick fruit and vegetables from a garden, allotment or farm.

Some parents worry a lot about the food their child eats – small children can easily be labelled as 'faddy eaters' and the knowledge that the same child eats anything that is going at Grandma's house can be upsetting. Looking after children should not turn into a competition but rather a joyful cooperation. Most children are curious about how other people live and it may just be much easier for them to try new tastes outside the home, particularly if the grandparents are relaxed about what they eat.

Betty's story

Betty always arranged a special plate of foods when her grandchildren came to visit. She had one huge plate on which she would put lots of food – tiny pieces of vegetables, meats, breads, pasta, rice, salad, fruit, pickles and tiny cakes. When the grandchildren asked why they didn't have this at home she told them that she had lots of time to plan for visits and their parents had to feed them everyday. Her grandchildren still enjoyed the big plate treatment even when they were teenagers.

Drinks

- All children need to drink frequently particularly in hot weather.
- Youngsters can be very vulnerable to becoming dehydrated if they are racing around in the park, so packing up a drink is very helpful.
- Water is preferable as too many drinks marketed for children are full of sugar and are bad for their teeth.
- If you do give a toddler fruit juice be sure to dilute it with water first.

Overweight children

Recent statistics show an increasing trend towards excess weight during childhood both in the USA and UK. If your grandchild seems to be carrying extra weight you may be worried that they are at increased risk of heart disease and diabetes later in life. Perhaps more worrying to your grandchild is that they may be teased and bullied at school and lose out on friendships.

It is important to remember that most children become overweight through circumstances over which they have little control – the food that is served to them at home and at school, whether they walk to school or are driven by car etc. Some children may seldom play outside or take part in swimming, sports or games with other children. Once children become overweight they can become reluctant to do sports that require them to use changing rooms and showers and so get even less exercise and interaction with other children.

Grandparents' attitudes are important in supporting children to feel loved, wanted and valued for who they are and not how much they weigh. One way to help might be to spend time together sharing the kinds of games or sport you enjoy. Whether it be swimming, walking, skipping or dancing it may help to spark off a more active lifestyle for them and maybe for you as well. Discuss with their parents whether a gift of lessons in a new sport would be welcomed – if you live near enough, parents may appreciate an offer to take your grandchild and bring them back home after a sporting activity. Grandparents living further away might offer to fund activity holidays or camps for children during the school holidays.

It is best not to remark on your grandchild's weight or insist on cutting back on their food – rather use time with them to prepare new recipes together that include healthy food choices. If he or she usually eats a lot of fatty foods then explain calmly that in your home you eat different foods and refrain from criticizing their parents and/or their usual food choices. Food can be a source of comfort for children, particularly if they are feeling upset by events in the family such as hearing their family argue or the birth of a new baby. At times like these spend time listening to your grandchild and lead by example rather than commiserating over a tub of ice cream.

Stella's story

Stella visited her family in New York where they had recently relocated following a change of employment for the father. She was excited to be reunited with her three grandsons – she promised her eldest grandson Bobby she would take him and her daughter out for dinner on the first night of her visit. When she met him she was horrified to notice how much weight he had put on but nevertheless honoured her promise to let him choose his meal. All went well until a huge plate of hamburger and chips arrived and Bobby proceeded to smother it with tomato ketchup. Stella got very angry and told him he was an ugly, fat and greedy child. Bobby was upset and pointed out he had been allowed to choose for himself. He remained silent for the rest of the meal, leaving half of it. When he got home he asked his mum if he could be excused from seeing Grandma for the rest of her visit.

As Bobby became more independent he walked and cycled everywhere and became a very fit young man. Stella's fears that his life would be ruined by his overweight stature proved untrue and she is very proud of her grandson and his good looks. Stella could have raised her concerns privately with her daughter. She could, for instance, have guessed that he was missing his old friends and comfort eating.

Eating disorders

To know that a teenage grandchild is risking their health by either not eating or inducing vomiting after food is distressing for all the family. Sadly, girls are particularly vulnerable to becoming detached from a realistic view of their bodies, believing they are overweight despite becoming dangerously thin.

Any young person with an eating disorder is likely to need professional help which will include advising the wider family. Grandparents' unconditional love and support to all the family is the appropriate response – battles at mealtimes will not help at all. Offer help to their parents by helping them to understand it is not their fault, help them to cope with family life – your family may need some time for a break and perhaps you can offer to care for their family to enable them to get away from the pressures for a few days. Ask them how you can best help, they may just need your assurance that they are good, caring parents.

Food and religious observance

If your grandchildren are being raised in a family where their parents are from different faith backgrounds or have converted to a faith unfamiliar to you, explore with them what this means in practice. Individuals will choose to what degree their religion impacts on everyday life and the food they eat.

It is better to ask your son or daughter and their partner their opinion about the food their children will eat whilst sharing meals with you. Many grandparents in this situation enjoy participating in religious festivals unfamiliar to them and grandchildren will thrive when both sets of grandparents share in the foods of both cultures.

If particular foods are taboo for religious reasons ask your family to advise on a list of unsuitable items and keep them well out of reach of your grandchildren.

Vegetarians and vegans

The growing numbers of vegetarian and vegan parents will want their children to follow their choice of diet. Ask for help in choosing food and cooperate in expanding a range of new dishes to serve to all family members. Meals may go much better if everyone eats the same food rather than risk the dislike of some vegans and vegetarians seeing others eating meat. Ensure that big occasions such as Christmas or Thanksgiving festivities have good vegetarian options even if pressure of tradition means there is a roast turkey available.

Question:

My grandchildren have decided to become vegetarians and they will no longer eat meat. Isn't this bad for them?

Answer:

It is very easy for vegetarians to eat a healthy, balanced diet. Most libraries and bookshops have a wide choice of vegetarian cookery books. Perhaps you could plan to cook a new menu together next time they visit.

Checklist

1 Be advised on diet by the parents.
2 Do not introduce salt or sugar into the diets of young children.
3 Take the risk of allergy seriously – no peanuts.
4 Offer young children frequent drinks particularly in warm weather.
5 Do not insist that all food is eaten.
6 Offer alternative treats to sweets – e.g. soft fruits or small gifts such as crayons.

06

money matters

In this chapter you will learn:
- the best way to save money for your grandchildren
- whether you should give financial help to your children
- tips on giving pocket money and gifts.

Banks, building societies and other financial institutions involved in researching how people spend their money are regularly producing evidence that increasing numbers of grandparents are financially assisting their adult children and their grandchildren. These reports show that when parents struggle to make ends meet their own parents are putting their hands deep in their pockets to make up the shortfall.

The amounts of money changing hands within families include substantial sums towards buying homes, paying for childcare, repaying loans or saving for school or university costs. The grandparents may want to buy expensive gifts of furniture, white goods (washing machines and dishwashers) and/or baby equipment. This trend to help goes back centuries but may have been accelerated by many of the baby boomer generation having dual income households, working longer and having experienced record rises in the value of their own homes. In more affluent societies families' gifts to younger family members of newly purchased items may be more prevalent than in the past when handed down items were more common.

For the younger generation, particularly in the UK, the twenty-first century has seen the purchase of a first home become out of reach for many couples, let alone single parents. The prospect of repaying large mortgages and accumulated debt from college or university means family money management faces a substantial challenge as babies enter the equation. Some couples may have got into debt to fund infertility treatment or private pre-natal and maternity care.

Giving financial help to your children

There is ample evidence that money can be at the heart of many marital rows and family feuds; perhaps loaning or giving money should come with a health warning. Whatever the reason you wish to help your adult child you may want to work through the checklist at the end of this chapter before you make any financial commitments.

Even with the best intentions a gift or loan of money is likely to change the nature of your relationships with both the child you have gifted money to and their siblings. Such gifts could also trigger disagreements between you and your partner so be well advised to discuss your proposed generosity well in advance of making any offers. If you are in a relationship sit down with your partner and talk through your finances, joint and individual. It may be helpful to talk through both the practical and emotional aspects of parting with large sums of money. Depending on your circumstances, making a large loan may make a substantial impact to your own lifestyle. You may want to take the chance of reviewing thoroughly your own finances and savings for retirement.

Harry and Nesta's story

When Harry and Nesta's son Will decided to marry his university sweetheart, Katy, they were overjoyed. The young couple had saved some money but were nowhere near being able to buy their own home. When Katy became pregnant a year after the wedding Harry and Nesta dug into their retirement savings to help the couple buy a small house. Harry and Nesta were shocked when their son asked to come and stay with them when their grandson was two years old. It turned out that Katy had asked for a divorce and Will needed to stay in his childhood home while he found somewhere else to live. Three years later, divorced and struggling financially, he is still living with his parents.

Some families may get into debt through lifestyle choices that may include use of drugs, alcohol or large credit card debt. If this is the situation in your family, giving or lending money may only exacerbate the problem. You may need support to say 'no' to the demands for your help – contacting agencies that give support to families in these situations may help you stay strong and cope with the practical and emotional strains these problems put on families.

Giving financial help to your grandchildren

Many grandparents will want to save some money specifically for their grandchildren. Even modest amounts of money put aside early in life can help young people to learn the importance of saving and enable them to have a lump sum to assist them at 18 or 21. It is helpful for family harmony to ensure that the sum you put aside to start their savings is the same for all your grandchildren and future grandchildren.

Savings accounts

Most banks and building societies have accounts that have been designed for children's savings which may have good rates of interest compared with adult savings accounts.

Banks want to woo their young customers and may send them fun items and an annual birthday card. As with other types of savings it is worth shopping around for the best rate of interest and changing the account if the rates lag behind. The finance pages of newspapers, magazines, TV, radio and internet sites will often carry articles comparing accounts by a number of different providers. Such information changes frequently, do consult a financial advisor when investing large sums of money.

Children's accounts can be used flexibly with any member of the family able to contribute either on an occasional basis or by a regular gift arrangement. Some children enjoy knowing that they have some money of their own and it's a great idea to talk to them about managing money and putting money aside for things they may want to buy or do in the future. You may like to discuss with other members of the family who will have the adult signature on the account and for what purposes money may be drawn out before the grandchild reaches 18 years of age.

Clinton and Daisy's story

Clinton and Daisy's children were the first generation of their family to go to university and get degrees. Clinton and Daisy had helped as much as they could and their children had taken out loans to help fund their studies. When they sold their large family home to move into a small apartment they decided to use some of their money to set up a university fund for each of their grandchildren and set some money aside just in case there were any more grandchildren to come.

Children's pensions

It's hard to imagine your grandchild reaching retirement but you probably already know that the later you start saving the harder it is to afford a good standard of living in retirement. One choice you can make is to ensure your grandchild benefits from a pension – there is no lower age limit to the age you can start one but your grandchild will need to be at least 55 years old before the pension savings can be spent. An advantage of some pension schemes is that they may be a very tax efficient way of saving and your grandchild may start adding some money themselves once they have started work.

Pocket money

Receiving regular pocket money is a useful way of learning to manage money. Some parents and grandparents may find it hard to resist the 'pester power' of young children to receive pocket money. This 'pester power' in addition to the many marketing campaigns result in children in the UK receiving an estimated £75 million a week in pocket money.

If you know your grandchild is saving up for a big ticket item you could offer, with agreement of the parent, to add to their savings when they have reached a certain amount as a reward for their effort to save.

Christmas and birthday presents

It may be hard to decide on an appropriate present for your grandchild and you may be tempted to provide cash instead. Do discuss this with their parents, it may be they may need some financial help to buy a joint family present or help to pay for a birthday party.

In the excitement of opening presents and birthday cards it is easy for young children to lose a cheque, voucher or bank note. It might be more fun to put on offer a visit with the grandchild to their favourite store so they can choose with you the item of their choice within an agreed budget. This enables you to enjoy helping them choose and share the excitement of a new toy. If the toy or book they want is below your budget help them put the change into their savings account.

Magazine and subscriptions

A subscription to a comic or magazine is an excellent way to interest a young child in reading and the arrival of a regular gift will be exciting all the year around. A number of publications support a child's interest in a particular television programme and many have activities for children that support their learning. Alternatively, many charities have developed junior membership schemes that both benefit the charity and also encourage an interest in their topic such as wildlife conservation. These charities may also send out regular child-friendly mailings.

Supporting charities

You may like to encourage your grandchild's interest in helping other people by working with them to raise money for their favourite charity by doing a sponsored event together – such as a scavenger hunt.

Many children also enjoy finding 'pre-owned' toys and books at charity shops, jumble sales and summer fêtes. Such finds cost a fraction of their price in the shops and can be recycled again once they are discarded.

Increasingly, charities are collecting a wide range of gifts that will make a big difference to children in need.

Piggy banks

Keeping a piggy bank for small change is a traditional way of ensuring that 'by looking after the pennies, the pounds will look after themselves'. Perhaps you could keep one at your home and make a tradition of counting the money when your grandchild visits. Counting the coins can assist your grandchild with their mathematic skills and also to learn the value of money. Attitudes to money are shaped early in life and maybe a shared philosophy of dividing the coins into two piles – one to save and one to spend – could influence their interest in saving.

Leaving money to your family

Help your family to deal with your finances after your death by seeking advice from a financial advisor and a solicitor regarding the best way to ensure your estate is divided up to reflect your wishes. By writing a will you are ensuring your wishes are followed. Sometimes wills have to be revised during your lifetime to reflect changes in the family situation, be sure to do this if this is the case.

Checklist

1 Give only as much as you can afford.
2 Discuss gifts and loans with your partner.
3 Encourage your grandchildren to save money for their future.
4 Get financial advice before making big decisions.
5 Make a will.

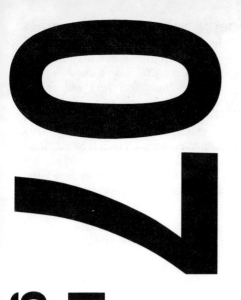

07

long-distance grandparenting

In this chapter you will learn:
- how to manage visits to your grandchildren
- how to make the most of visits from your family
- how to keep a scrapbook of family memories.

Nowadays many families have grandchildren and grandparents living in different parts of the world. The birth of a new baby can be the final realization that a tentative move may become more permanent as the new family start to raise a child in their adopted home. Some grandparents may feel very sad at the prospect of a new generation growing up far away from them and wonder how family relationships will develop in future. However, the long distance grandparents may develop very close and important bonds with their grandchildren by working with their parents to plan enjoyable visits, talk on Skype (see Appendix 1, p. 137), exchange emails, photos, news and gifts; and can learn from each other the best times and ways to communicate.

Distance and gaps between visits can enhance the joys of meeting up – and each visit can create happy memories for all concerned if handled sensitively.

When your family move

Grandparents may experience mixed emotions when families move cities or go to another country. The move may well result from promotion in a job or the chance to create a better quality of life for your grandchildren. However pleased they are for their children some grandparents describe feeling a sense of bereavement; particularly if the distance means visits are likely to be infrequent. If the grandparents have regularly cared for the grandchildren, their leaving will create a gap that may be hard to come to terms with. Talking to friends in similar situations can be a great source of comfort as can contacting the helpline at the Grandparents' Association or local support network.

Nora and Tom's story

Nora and Tom have grandchildren who live on the other side of the Atlantic to them. Whenever they visit a book shop they buy two copies of the most exciting-looking children's books. They mail one copy to their grandchildren and when the books arrive they arrange a Skype call to their family. The grandchildren then look at the same book while Nora or Tom read it aloud.

Julie's story

Julie often makes transatlantic visits to her two grandsons. In between visits she finds it useful to plan her telephone conversations with her grandchildren. She keeps a notebook in which she jots down key details such as the names of their teachers and their friends and makes sure she asks questions to keep track of their interests and activities.

Managing visits to your family

- Planning visits well in advance can ease the costs by enabling families to shop around for cheap fares.

- If the dates of your visit may be subject to change it is advisable to shop around for tickets which allow you to change plans. To have a degree of flexibility it may be well worth paying a little extra rather than buying the cheapest ticket. This could be particularly important if you are planning to be around for the birth of your grandchild – as dates can never be guaranteed.

- If you are looking for long-distance flights you may like to plan your visits at times when most people are not on holiday. November and February can be very much cheaper than other months.

- Flying to be together at Christmas can be very expensive but prices are often dramatically lower if you can wait until 26th December to depart.

- Some grandparents recognize that it may be easier for all concerned to stay near their family in a local guest house or hotel. It is well worth discussing this option if you can afford it – both generations get a break from each other and there is space to unwind. However, talk about it so that your family is not upset if you choose not to stay in their home.

- A low cost alternative is to house swap with a family who live near to your own family. Although many websites cater for this need you may get better results from local websites and newsletters or through your family's network of friends.

Outstaying your welcome

How long to stay is another sensitive question for some grandparents who may worry about outstaying their welcome and putting future visits at risk. Discussions can ease the situation and so can a reassurance that the younger generation do not need to spend their every waking minute with you.

Plan to do some activities on your own – including perhaps a short sightseeing trip in the middle of your visit. As your grandchild gets older you may want to encourage the parents to use your babysitting services whilst you are staying and even to take a short holiday themselves.

Many grandparents enjoy being on their own with the grandchildren and getting to know them better away from the watchful, and occasionally critical, eyes of their parents. If you do babysit ensure you are fully briefed and have all telephone numbers to hand and instructions on the location of key items including favourite toys and food.

Managing visits from your family

Family visits will need plenty of preparation particularly when there are babies or small children coming to stay in your home.

- It's wise to check carefully on the needs of the youngest generation before the family arrive.
- Much that you need may be available second-hand or can be borrowed from friends. The National Childbirth Trust (UK) regularly holds clothes and equipment sales to raise funds and local charity or thrift shops will often have bargains.
- Toys can also be borrowed from a local toy library or from friends for the duration of a visit.
- If the family use terry-towelling nappies you may want to check out a local nappy laundering service for the forthcoming visit.
- Make sure that a supply of disposable nappies is exactly the right make and size – your grandchild will probably have changed sizes between visits.
- Realize that the family may want to use their time back in their old community to reconnect with their friends, siblings and other relatives. If this is the situation in your household, rather than feeling put upon, do some advance planning which balances time spent with you and that spent with other people.

- The parent generation may appreciate a lie-in while you watch over the grandchild, or have time that is child-free to go out together as a couple.
- Likewise, you may need to know that on certain days your house will be quiet whilst the family go out and you can have some time to rest up.
- The short time your family have to be with you may cast a shadow on the visit and you may resent their friends at times. Remember, the more they enjoy their visit the sooner you are likely to see them again. Tell your adult children what is working well for you – if they are finding it difficult seeing lots of friends you might suggest giving a party for them. That way you may find that you enjoy catching up with their friends too.
- Older children may find it difficult to be away from their friends at home – you may like to find out about local activities for your grandchildren to enjoy. You may also want to ask around and find friends and neighbours who have similar age children in the family.

Top tip

Don't make your children feel guilty about their choices. They will have their own reasons for choosing a particular place to live with their growing children. Trust their judgement and try not to ask when they are going to move nearer to you – that's up to them.

Family holidays

A number of families share a week's annual holiday – often the same week at the same place every year. Each adult sibling and their family pay for their own self-catering accommodation and the adults take turns to cater and babysit. The advantage is that no one feels overcrowded and the size of chalet/cottage/villa can change each year as families grow and shrink. Places chosen are usually family resorts with plenty of activities and within the price range of all concerned. Many children enjoy the opportunity of being part of a larger family group for a short while and the sense of continuity an annual trip provides.

Creating memories

One way you can create happy memories for you and your grandchild is to buy scrapbooks to record together the things you have done together, whether it be at their home or at yours. Photographs, tickets, postcards, drawing around hands/feet, height measurements, autographs and anecdotes can all be recorded and revisited on the next trip.

However, it's not always necessary to wait until the next visit. Sticking a picture in the family album can now be an activity shared globally with family members. It is not only in paper scrapbooks that pictures can be kept but also in virtual albums or in scrapbooks on a computer. These can then be emailed between grandchild and grandparent or a family archive set up.

A growing interest in family history and genealogy can be shared using the World Wide Web together with contact details for all the family. Create a safe space with a password protecting the space from all but family members. The role of webmaster and resident techie can include help to ensure that any member of the family without internet access can be sent updates by post. Each family member can contribute to create a virtual family archive.

The advent of the internet, web cameras and Skype all facilitate the talking and sharing of news between grandparents and their child and grandchildren. The lines of communication and information sharing are ever increasing.

Sarah's story

Susan has one son living in England with teenage children, a second son in South Africa and a daughter living in the USA with one small boy of eight years old and twin boys of six. She gets an enormous amount of pleasure being involved with her grandchildren and watching them grow up. However, it comes at a price – all too often the parting at an airport is very emotional. The children insist on knowing when she will next return. The family has to make arrangements from one visit to the next, trying not to leave until the next visit, at home or abroad, is at least tentatively planned. She also has to give serious consideration to the extra travelling expenses, although she tries to balance this mentally against the frequent outings she would be able to offer them if they lived nearby in her home town.

Sarah keeps careful records of all gifts and treats for her grandchildren. She ensures that, as far as possible, she provides equal treatment, presents and trips for all of them.

From the point of view of her grandchildren in the USA, she is aware that she should not go on a crash-course spoiling them, or let the visit, because short, become too intense. Instead, she tries to enjoy every day as it comes, not thinking too much that it may be as much as a year before they next meet – there is always the telephone after all! She also has become an accomplished user of Skype and emails, helped by courses at her local community centre and coaching from her grandchildren.

Multilingual families

If your grandchild is being raised with a different mother tongue to your own you can be assured that babies and young children respond well to different languages; bilingual children have been shown to do very well at learning other languages in later life. An effort on your part to learn the language of your grandchildren can be very rewarding – and you may then enjoy sharing both languages with your grandchild.

Checklist

1 Ensure you put a brave face on periods of separation and don't take their move as a personal slight.
2 Plan to do fun activities with your grandchildren when they are with you. Pre-book tickets to avoid wasting time queuing.
3 Send post cards, emails, photographs and little surprises in the post.
4 Shop around for good deals on travel and consider travelling outside the holiday season.
5 Get out and about and enjoy other aspects of your life – explore new interests you can share with your family.

08

having fun with your grandchild

In this chapter you will learn:
- how to amuse children on a rainy day
- the best ways of having outdoor fun
- tips on finding ideas for day trips
- how to choose appropriate toys.

Grandparents are often in an ideal position as they can enjoy all the fun of spending time with their grandchildren without having most of the responsibilities that go with being a parent. Grandchildren often see their grandparents as people who it is fun to be with and spending time with their grandparents will often be one of their favourite things to do.

Read on for a few ideas and activities for having fun with your grandchildren.

Rainy day fun

Just because it's pouring down with rain outside doesn't mean that your grandchildren have to be bored. Although putting a favourite video on for younger children can sometimes be a lifesaver, if it's too cold or wet to go out to play there's no need to sit in front of the TV all day.

When the grandchildren cry out that familiar line 'I'm bored!'; why not try some of the following activities?

Baking

- Grandparents can teach even the youngest child the basics of cooking and the enjoyment that children get out of eating something that they have made themselves is often worth all the mess!
- Measuring and mixing ingredients to bake some fairy cakes or biscuits and decorating them can keep young children amused on a rainy day and they can even help you with the washing-up!
- If you can't face the thought of flour everywhere, children can have fun and learn about cooking by helping you prepare their own food, by buttering their own bread, and choosing and chopping up healthy fillings for sandwiches.
- Although the idea of jam and cucumber sandwiches may not be too appetizing to everyone, even the most fussy of eaters may be willing to try new foods if they have made it themselves.

Music

- Listening to music and dancing together can be great fun and good exercise for both children and grandparents.

- Nursery rhymes or popular songs can be sung together and can be even more fun if accompanied by appropriate noises and actions. Pick up a supply of children's music CDs from your local library.
- Those favourite songs that you sang with your own children will come flooding back and may become firm favourites with your grandchildren.
- Babies and young children may enjoy listening to your CD collection and you can even teach them some of your long-forgotten dance moves.
- This works both ways though, and older children may like to show you the kind of music they listen to. You may even learn some new dance moves as well!

Family history

- Young children will often be interested in their own family history, for example, listening to family stories inspired by old photos of their parents or even your own childhood snaps.
- Older grandchildren love hearing funny stories about their own parents' and grandparents' childhood and if they are really keen you can even make a simple family tree together or delve deeper and try to trace your family history.

The great outdoors

Children love being outside in the fresh air; here are a few ideas for having fun outside.

Gardening

- Whether you only have a small window box or a huge sprawling garden, you can still enjoy getting green-fingered with your grandchildren.
- Children love being outside and most enjoy getting their hands dirty. Gardening with your grandchild can be great fun. From digging and raking, planting and watering to picking the fruits or vegetables, children can learn a great deal.
- Whether you are growing tomatoes, carrots or tulips or even just some cress seeds on a windowsill, grandparents can help their grandchildren understand about looking after plants and why they need water and sunlight to grow.

- If you can spare the space, children can enjoy having their own little patch of garden to look after.
- When it comes to harvesting their crop, children often feel a great sense of achievement that they have grown something and will often be more willing to try out new fruit and vegetables if they have planted, looked after and picked them themselves.

Water fun

- Although young children must be supervised at all times around water, on a warm day try filling up a washing up bowl with some water and giving the grandchildren a few plastic cups, jugs and containers for filling and emptying.
- Once they are finished playing they can use what's left to help water the garden.
- If you don't have access to a garden your grandchild will enjoy sitting in a bath with lots of water toys.

Out and about

You may decide on occasions to take your grandchildren outside your home but may be worried about the expense and organization. Don't be. You don't need to spend a small fortune on a fun day out with your grandchildren and it need not be a military operation.

- Although trips to the cinema and theme parks are great places for a special day out, they can become very expensive if you add on extras such as popcorn and ice creams. If you do decide to go for a special treat, take your own drinks and snacks.
- Alternatively, choose a park or community event, your grandchildren will find a cheap day out can be just as much fun.
- Look in your local library, community centre or 'What's on' section of your local newspaper for events or places to visit in your area.
- If you don't drive go by the bus or train. Even if you drive everywhere, try leaving the car at home as young children often love the novelty of going on a train or riding on a bus if they usually travel everywhere in the back of a car.

• The publication *Let's go with the children* (UK) or the many children's guides to cities in the UK and North America have a lot of good ideas for days out with the grandchildren.

Park life

• A trip to your local park can be one of the most fun days out for grandchildren. Young children love being outdoors and need a safe play area to explore and run around.
• Take some food to feed the ducks along with a picnic and if your local green space doesn't have any play equipment take a ball or a frisbee for a fun day out!

Museums

• Some museums are free or charge only a small entrance fee and have a lot of 'hands on' activities or exhibitions designed to interest young children.
• Children will often enjoy being shown the same museums you visited with their parents as small children – seeing the same exhibits will give them lots to talk about when they get home as well.

Libraries

• Your library is an ideal place to help plan some fun activities to share with your grandchildren – your local children's librarian will be able to help you choose suitable books, videos and CDs to borrow.
• Many libraries run story time sessions for young children and some offer reading clubs for older children.
• If you don't have a personal computer at home, most libraries now have computers with internet access that can be used to help older grandchildren with homework.
• Many areas also have toy libraries that lend out toys to take home.

Harold and Lucy's story

Harold and Lucy have a long tradition of inviting their grandchildren to stay at half-term week. In preparation Harold searches the internet and Lucy collects leaflets from the library. On the first morning the children each get to choose one activity they would like to do during the week and Harold and Lucy also choose a favourite activity. At the end of each day the children write and draw a diary to leave between visits. They both love reading the diaries when the children are back at school.

Harold and Lucy also have a big toy box which they regularly replenish by shopping at yard sales so there are new toys for the children at each visit.

Choosing toys

When choosing toys for your grandchild and when thinking about what sort of play activities are suitable, it's important to consider the age of your grandchild to make sure that the types of activities and toys available are safe and appropriate for their age.

- Check that any toys or books picked up at yard sales, thrift shops or jumble sales are clean and safe before giving them to your grandchildren.
- It's a good idea before buying to check that any play equipment holds a CE mark which conforms to essential safety requirements and that toys hold the Lion Mark (in the UK), which is a recognizable consumer symbol that denotes safety and quality. In addition, try to make sure that any products with age warnings such as 'not suitable for under three years old' are appropriate for the age of your grandchild.
- Although there is a lot of choice these days when shopping for toys, you don't need to spend a lot of money and sometimes the simplest toys and household objects are the best. It's only too true that children are often more interested in the box that the toys came in and the latest craze for a particular toy doesn't usually last long.
- It's also best to check with the parents before buying new toys, especially in the case of things such as toy guns or swords.

Here are a few ideas if you are thinking about buying your grandchild a toy or are planning some activities that are appropriate for their age:

New babies

Toys that can be explored with fingers or mouths such as rattles, soft toys in different fabrics and objects to help babies become more aware of their surroundings such as mobiles and music to listen to.

Babies from three months

Babies from about three months of age will be more active and will need the opportunity to strengthen their muscles and increase control over their head, eyes, hands and feet. Good toys for this age are soft balls or toys, rattles, teethers and clean, sterilized household objects such as wooden spoons or plastic bowls.

Crawling babies

Crawling babies need a safe space to explore. Good toys at this age include activity centres and mats; buckets, boxes and baskets to fill; toy bricks to build and knock down; simple posting boxes; pop-up toys; cars to push about and simple picture books. And a grandparent to share them with of course!

Toddlers

Children who are just starting to walk need space to move around in without getting knocked over and with large equipment that will safely help them to get their balance.

At this stage, children will enjoy toys that they can push and pull such as baby walkers to push (not the 'sit in' type as they are considered dangerous) and push-along toys such as prams, animals and 'pretend' machines such as toy vacuum cleaners.

Pre-school children

From around 18 months, children can enjoy a wide range of fun activities that can help their development.

> **Top tip**
>
> Some of these play activities will require more planning and supervision, particularly in the case of 'messy play' and water play.

The following types of toys will be enjoyed by pre-school children:

- Drawing and painting.
- Dressing-up clothes.
- Toy prams and dolls; toy telephones, cookers, vacuums; simple train sets, trucks and cars; toy animals.
- Bright, attractive picture books; stories about familiar events and situations. Listening to and re-telling stories can help to develop children's language.
- Bought or home-made play dough (see Appendix 2, p. 139), sand in a sand tray or washing-up bowl; water in a washing-up bowl; an assortment of plastic containers.
- Toddler-size slide and/or small climbing frame; large cardboard boxes; rocking horse or rocking chair; sit-and-ride toys; play tunnels.
- Plastic bricks, blocks and shapes; lacing and threading; peg board with pegs; shape sorters; toys to screw and turn.

Checklist

These quick tips are either free (or very cheap!) and will provide plenty of enjoyment for you and your grandchildren.

1 Keep a small collection of crayons, felt-tip pens, pencils, children's glue, safety scissors and paper for your grandchildren to use for creating some wonderful works of art when they visit.

2 Keep a special drawer, cupboard or shelf for your grandchildren's favourite games such as Scrabble, Snakes and Ladders or jigsaw puzzles.

3 Everyday chores such as shopping can be a good way for your grandchild to practise their reading, writing and numeracy skills by looking at labels on packaging, writing a shopping list and adding up at the till.

Even washing day can be fun by getting children to sort through the laundry and learn their colours.

4 Most children love stories. Tell them stories about your family and your own childhood. Also tell them about the toys and games that you may have played with as a child.

5 Dig out the old favourite books that you used to read to your own children and read them all over again with your grandchildren.

6 Help your grandchildren to practise their counting by keeping a small piggy bank with different amounts of coins to add up and save.

7 If you have a computer at home, store learning games on it, or look for learning websites. Older grandchildren can even teach their grandparents how to email them and how to design a simple website.

8 When watching TV together, talk about what is happening in the programme.

9 Young children love dressing-up. Try creating a dressing-up box from your old clothes and shoes or even visit a jumble sale or charity shop for dressing-up outfits.

10 Give your grandchildren some stamped addressed envelopes or postcards so that they can write to you or send you drawings and letters when you are apart.

Above all, have fun and make the most of every opportunity with your grandchildren.

09

helping your grandchildren to learn and communicate

In this chapter you will learn:
- how to help your grandchildren learn to read and count
- how to use games for learning
- how to listen to your grandchild
- what are the signs of difficulty in communicating.

It might be as little as fifteen years since you left full-time schooling or it might be nearer fifty, but one thing is certain, schools have changed since you were a pupil. This chapter is all about nursery and primary schools: what they do; how they do it; and how you can help whether you live near to your grandchildren or not.

Schooling progression

All children in the UK are entitled to a nursery place from their third birthday and they go to a primary school somewhere between their fourth and fifth birthday. The nursery years are called the 'early years foundation stage', and primary schools teach children at what is now called 'key stage 1' and 'key stage 2' (this is the case in England, Wales and Northern Ireland – Scotland has its own distinctive and flexible qualification framework that is separate from the National Curriculum).

Sometimes early years foundation stage classes are held in schools or Sure start or head start units, but private nurseries and playgroups are included too. They're known as 'settings'. The UK government has made sure that there is a good supply of places for children from birth up to five years old, and all settings are inspected regularly to check that what they're providing for young children is correct.

Whichever early years setting children go to, the adults who work there are all expected to organize the days in a similar way. The important thing is that they must provide interesting, fun and stimulating things for your grandchildren to do that are based on play. That includes playing outside as well as inside, painting, messy play, playing with water or paint, climbing, building things, riding bikes, playing with a ball or make-believe and dressing-up. This stage ends with the reception year and this will always be part of a school – either an infant school, or a primary school.

Key stage 1 includes what are now called Year 1 and Year 2. Children are between five and seven in key stage 1 and in the grandparent's day it was probably called the infant department. The junior school (if it's a separate school), or junior department (if it's part of a primary school) covers Year 3 to Year 6. Children are seven or eight in Year 3 and ten or 11 in Year 6. Then they move into secondary school and compulsory schooling goes on until they reach the end of Year 11 when they're fifteen or very nearly sixteen.

Home schooling

Your grandchildren may be among those whose parents are choosing to educate them at home. If so, you may want to find out how you can learn about home education and work with the parents to see if you can perhaps help them to teach your grandchildren.

A list of organizations that have resources on support for home schooling are suggested in the Taking it further section.

Subjects

Literacy

So, what will your grandchildren learn in these all-important first few years of schooling? Reading, writing and maths are taught every day, and the children are taught each in the best way to suit them at the stage they're at. Children in the early years foundation stage and key stage 1 will be taught to read and write using phonics. The best way to find out more about this is to ask at the school because there is a variety of different published ways of teaching it. Phonics is a way of using letter sounds to break down words for reading and to build up words for writing. Handwriting will be taught as well, and some schools teach 'joined up writing', or 'cursive script' from the start, while others wait until children have become confident with printing individual letters separately. This work is called literacy and you may hear your grandchildren talk about their literacy lessons.

Numeracy

Numeracy is what the children will call mathematics and it includes arithmetic, early geometry and some basic algebra. They might call these aspects 'shape work', and they'll probably tell you about 'problem-solving activities' as well. It should still sound as if they've been playing when they tell you what they've been doing in the early years foundation stage and Year 1 or Year 2, and even at the end of key stage 2, when they are in Year 6, much of their learning will involve playing games.

Communication

Something about schools that has changed a great deal over the last few years is that talking is now both encouraged and expected! One of the ways you can help even before your grandchildren go to either nursery or school, as well as when they get there, is to listen to them and to talk to them as much as possible. A famous psychologist called James Britton said, way back in the 1960s, that 'Reading and writing float on a sea of talk'. He meant that if children find it hard to talk and listen they won't do as well when it comes to learning literacy and numeracy at school. This is sometimes called 'communication', and it improves with practice at home and at school.

Very often grandparents can give grandchildren time to develop their communication skills when sometimes the parents may have less time to give. Just let the children go at their own pace, while you show interest and ask 'chatty' questions while helping them to learn about politeness such as taking turns and helping each other. An average four year old can ask as many as 600 'Why?' questions a day, and grandparents might have more time – and patience! – to answer them and help them to understand and learn about their world. Nobody expects you to be a teacher, but your support will help them to make the best progress at nursery and school.

When the grandchildren are with you, the best approach is just to do ordinary things together and encourage their talk and interest to grow. You might go to the park, or do some cooking; you could be making a meal or planting some seeds; you could possibly go to a museum or join the library. And grandparents are always good for long board games or reading books. Telling stories is a wonderful way of getting conversation going, and also learning about family history, especially if you start with things like, 'I remember when your Mummy/Daddy was six, (or eight, or ten) and …'. All these everyday activities help children with literacy, communication and numeracy.

Intergenerational learning

You will certainly learn from your grandchildren. How many times do adults ask younger people to help with the programming, say, of the DVD player, or the downloading of music onto an iPod? Many grandchildren help their elders in this kind of way, and it all helps relationships to develop as well as introducing the idea of intergenerational learning.

If you don't see your grandchildren very often you can write to them, text them, send them stories, drawings, photographs or poems, and also talk to them on the phone, via email. Encourage them – or their parents on their behalf – to send you pictures, paintings and stories in the post too. Sometimes you might even be lucky enough to be able to use a webcam together and see each other as you talk.

If you're invited to go to your grandchildren's school, perhaps to a grandparents' assembly or open day, it's likely that the school will have organized activities that you can share with your grandchild throughout the day – even to the extent of having a school lunch together! These opportunities can help to give you an understanding of what goes on in early years settings or schools these days and how the teachers work, and they will welcome your questions.

Resources for grandparents

The Basic Skills Agency in the UK has worked with the Grandparents' Association, Grandparents Plus and Goldsmiths College to produce a series of resources and material for grandparents of early years foundation stage and primary grandchildren. You can see them by visiting the website at **www.basic-skills.co.uk,** and following the links to either publications, early years or primary. Alternatively, the Grandparents' Association website, at **www.grandparents-association.org.uk,** and Grandparents Plus at **www.grandparentsplus.org,** each have links and separate resources to help you.

If you want to know more about the early years foundation stage or primary schools, the Department for Education and Skills website, **www.standards.dfes.gov.uk,** will lead you in the right direction. There are 'frequently asked questions' pages for early years and each key stage.

A good practice guide for schools, *Learning with grandparents: Grandparents and schools working together to support basic skills development,* by Ian Gyllenspetz, produced by the Basic Skills Agency, makes the following recommendations about getting involved with your grandchildren's learning:

1 Do as much with your grandchild as you possibly can. Each meeting is a learning experience for them and strengthens the emotional bond between you.

2 Do not try to be a teacher – just be a loving grandparent who is interested in and likes being with their grandchildren. Have fun and learn together.

3 Ask your grandchildren's parents for any information the school sends out about events and the work the children are doing. Letters to families include you, especially if you're sharing the caring.

4 If you can go to assemblies, courses and workshops, you'll get to know what's going on and keep up to date. Do talk to the literacy and numeracy teachers – they'll tell you a lot more!

5 Try to help the school if you can – listening to readers is a favourite. It doesn't have to be your grandchildren's school if you don't live near, you'll be welcomed wherever you are. You might offer to share your experiences or skills such as cooking or gardening with the children too.

6 If you drop off or collect your grandchildren from school, take the chance to talk to their teachers and ask to have a look around. Your grandchildren will be proud to show you their classroom and school.

7 Try to support your grandchildren's learning whenever and however you can. Going on a school trip with them can be a great experience and it helps the teachers at the same time.

8 Talk to other grandparents you might meet at the school – you might find that there are special courses or workshops you can all do together to find out more about how children learn and how you can be an even greater support to them.

9 You might enrol on a learning course yourself! If you have learning needs, don't be afraid to ask what's on offer, it could make a huge difference to your life. In many Children's Centres or new Extended Schools, there are family learning staff who will be happy to advise. The Basic Skills Agency and the Grandparents' Association have developed some courses especially written for grandparents (see Taking it further).

10 You have an important role to play in the lives of your grandchildren so don't be afraid to ask questions or to ask for help. We all continue to learn and it does show the children and the families how much you care. Sometimes a grandparent is the one who is providing stability for the whole family.

11 If you are a grandad, get involved – the school and the children often need more men to help.

12 Visit the school's website if it has one – they're often very informative.

Finally, look out for a set of Basic Skills Agency, Goldsmiths College, Grandparents Plus and Grandparents' Association resources with pictures of 'Grandducks' on them. One in particular, 'A jargon-busting ABC of primary schools', describes in more detail how early years settings and primary schools work. It includes a list of terms and words that may be new to you and covers education in the twenty-first century. A set of 'Good practice cards' goes with a short DVD which shows ordinary grandparents doing ordinary activities with their grandchildren, pointing out what they're doing to help with literacy and numeracy development. There is a set of postcards that grandparents and grandchildren can send to each other, and two booklets called 'It doesn't take much to keep in touch', and 'Things to do when you're apart', which offer tips on how to develop a relationship with grandchildren who don't live very close by.

All the resources are produced for you, to help you in supporting your grandchildren's learning. The activities in them are fun, interesting, inexpensive, easy to organize and will definitely help your young grandchildren to become confident in literacy and numeracy as they grow up.

Communication stages

Children learn language by interacting with other people. There is a wide variation in the rate at which children develop communication (including speech and language). Some children develop quickly while others may take a little more time. Often, children who are slow to develop these skills initially soon catch up with other children. But, for some children, developing communication can be a very difficult process and they may need extra help to develop their speech, language and communication skills. Grandparents can play an important part in supporting the development of speech and language skills and for many children are the first adult outside the family home with whom they can practise their speech and language.

Developing communication is a gradual process. Children begin to understand words before they can say them. They then learn how to say these words and how to put them together to make sentences. Children will learn a whole range of different sounds and use these and all their other skills to communicate with others. There are many ways that grandparents can encourage and support the development of communication at every stage of a child's life.

Stages of Speech and Language Development

	Listening and attention	Understanding	Speech sounds and talk	Social skills
Up to 3 months	• Turns towards a familiar sound • Startled by loud noises	• Recognizes parent's voice • Often calmed by familiar friendly voice, e.g. parent's voice	• Frequently cries, especially when unhappy or when uncomfortable • Makes vocal sounds, e.g. cooing, gurgling	• Gazes at facial movements, e.g. sticking out out tongue • Makes eye contact for fairly long periods
3–6 months	• Watches face when someone talks	• Shows excitement at sound of approaching voices	• Makes vocal noises to get attention • Makes sounds back when talked to • Laughs during play • Babbles to self	• Senses different emotions in parent's voice and may respond differently, for example, smile, quieten, laugh • Cries in different ways to express different needs
6–12 months	• Locates source of voice with accuracy • Focuses on different sounds, e.g. telephone, doorbell, clock	• Understands frequently used words such as 'all gone', 'no' and 'bye-bye'	• Uses speech sounds (babbling) to communicate with adults; says sounds like 'ba-ba no-no, go-go'	• Enjoys action rhymes and songs • Tries to copy adult speech and lip movements

		• Stops and looks when hears own name • Understands simple instructions when supported by gestures and context	• Stops babbling when hears a familiar adult voice • Uses gestures such as waving and pointing to help communicate • Around 12 months begins to use single words e.g. **'mummum'**, **'dada'**, **'tete'** (teddy)	• Takes 'turns' in conversations (using babble)
12–15 months	• Attends to music and singing • Enjoys sounds – making toys/objects	• Understands single words in context, e.g. cup, milk, daddy • Understands more words than they can say • Understands simple instructions, e.g. **'kiss mummy'**, **'give to daddy'**, **'stop'**	• Says around 10 single words although these may not be clear • Reaches or points to something they want whilst making speech sounds	• Likes being with familiar adults • Likes watching adults for short periods of time
15–18 months	• Listens and responds to simple information/ instructions, e.g. **'Ben, put on shoes'**, **'Mohammed, give to daddy'**	• Understands a wide range of single words and some two-word phrases, e.g. **'give me'**, **'shoe on'**	• Still babbles but uses at least 20 single words correctly, although may not be clear	• Simple pretend play • Plays alone, although likes to be near familiar adult

	Listening and attention	Understanding	Speech sounds and talk	Social skills
				• Although increasingly independent, happiest when near familiar adult
			• Copies gestures and words from adults • Constantly babbling and single words used during play • Uses intonation, pitch and changing volume when 'talking'	
18 months – 2 years	• Focuses on a activity of their own choice but finds it difficult to be directed by an adult • Use of child's name beginning to help them to attend to what an adult says, e.g. 'Sarah, eat sandwiches', 'Ali, put coat on'	• Understanding of single words develops rapidly during this stage: anything between 200 and 500 words are known • Understands more simple instructions, e.g. 'Get mummy's shoes', 'Get your bricks', 'Tell dad tea's ready'	• Uses up to 50 words • Begins to put two or three words together • Frequently asks questions, e.g. the names of people and objects (towards 2 years) • Uses speech sounds p, b, m, w	• 'Pretend' play developing with toys, such as feeding a doll or driving a car • Becomes frustrated when unable to make self understood – this may result in tantrums • Follows adult body language including pointing, gesture and facial expressions
2–3 years	• Beginning to listen to talk with interest, but easily distracted • Listens to talk addressed to him/herself, but finds it difficult if	• Developing understanding of simple concepts including in/on/under, big/little	• Uses 300 words including descriptive language, time, space, function • Links four to five words together	• Holds a conversation but jumps from topic to topic • Interested in other's and will join in

	Attention and listening	Understanding	Speech	Social
	• prompts are not provided, e.g. **use of name, 'stop and listen'**	• Understands phrases like **'put teddy in the box', 'get your book, coat and bag', 'draw a big brown dog'** • Understands simple **'who'** and **'what'** and **'where'** questions but not **'why'**	• May stutter or stammer when thinking what to say • Able to use pronouns (me, him, she), plurals and prepositions (in, on, under) • Has problems with saying speech sounds: l/r/w/y, f/th, s/sh/ch/dz/j	• Expresses emotions towards adults and or peers using words, not just actions
		• Understands a simple story when supported with pictures		
3–4 years	• Enjoys listening to stories • Still finds it difficult to attend to more than one thing at a time, so can't easily listen to a speaker whilst still carrying on an activity; has to switch attention between speaker and task	• Understands questions or instructions with two parts: **'get your jumper'** and **'stand by the door'** • Understands **'why'** questions • Aware of time in relation to past, present and future, e.g. **Today is sunny, yesterday was rainy. I wonder what the weather will be like tomorrow?** (towards four years)	• Uses sentences of four to six words, e.g. **'I want to play with cars', 'What's that thingy called?'** • Uses future and past tense • May continue to have problems with irregular words, **'runned'** for **'ran', 'swimmed'** for **'swam'** • Able to remember and enjoys telling long stories or singing songs	• Understands turn-taking as well as sharing with adults and peers • Initiates conversations • Enjoys playing with peers • Able to argue with adults or peers if they disagree – uses words, not just actions

	Listening and attention	Understanding	Speech sounds and talk	Social skills
			• Has problems with saying r, j, th, ch, and sh	
4–5 years	• Attention is now more flexible – the child can understand spoken instructions related to a task without stopping the activity to look at the speaker	• Able to follow simple story without pictures • Understands instructions containing sequencing words: '**first... after... last**' • Understands adjectives: **soft, hard, smooth,** etc. • Aware of more complex humour, laughs at jokes that are told	• Uses well formed sentences, e.g. '**I played with Ben at lunch time**' but there may still be some grammatical errors • Easily understood by adults and peers, with only a few immaturities in speech sounds, for example, '**th**', '**r**' and three consonant combinations '**scribble**' • Frequently asks the meaning of unfamiliar words and may use them randomly	• Chooses own friends • Generally cooperative with playmates • Able to plan construction and make believe play activities • Takes turns in longer conversations • Uses language to gain information, negotiate, discuss feelings/ideas and give opinions

Adapted from BT/I CAN resource *Learning to Talk, Talking to Learn*. I CAN is the children's communication charity.

Grandparents can help to develop these communication stages through pre-school, primary and early teenage years, although, of course, communication skills start right from birth.

Singing

Singing to and cooing at a new baby provides the starting point for communication development. Game playing and storytelling are also essential from the earliest age to encourage speaking and listening ability.

Nursery rhymes and songs have been sung for hundreds of years to entertain children or soothe them to sleep. Singing to and with grandchild also helps to develop their speech and language – from learning to pay attention and developing an enjoyment for listening to understanding about rhyme and developing prediction.

- There are lots of traditional songs that can be used to help develop speech, language and communication.
- If you sing action songs, children, especially younger ones, can join in with the actions long before they can join in with the words.
- If you don't know many songs or the ones that you do know you don't like, you can make them up – there are many songs that can be sung to the tune of 'Twinkle, twinkle, little star' or 'Frere Jaques'.
- Old MacDonald can have any number of people, animals, modes of transport, etc. on his farm. And adults and children stamping feet, clapping hands and shouting 'Hi' can all go along with 'The wheels on the bus'.

Playing games

Playing games with your grandchild is a great way to help him/her develop communication skills. The time and attention you give to them while playing will support other important skills too, like taking turns or counting. And you thought you were just having fun! These games cost very little, in fact, many use just your imagination or household objects. It's the playing and interacting with your grandchild that's the important part.

Kim's game

Resources:

- medium size tray
- number of small objects (key, pen, egg cup, toy car etc.)
- tea towel.

1 Collect a number of small objects – between four and eight depending on your grandchild's age.
2 Put the objects onto the tray and spend a few minutes talking about each object in turn.
3 Let your grandchild hold each object and encourage him or her to name each one and use a word to describe it, e.g. shiny key, red car, etc.
4 You can join in this part of the game too by taking it in turns to pick up and describe each object – giving good model communication and making the game more fun.
5 Cover the objects with the tea towel and remove one object without letting your grandchild see which one has been removed.
6 Remove the tea towel and ask, 'What has gone?' with a big smile.
7 Next time the objects are covered your grandchild removes an object and you have to work out what's missing.

I went to market and I bought...

This game can be played by any number of people but the more people the more things there are to remember. It's best to introduce this game when there are just the two of you.

1 You start off this game by saying, 'I went to market and I bought... e.g. a bottle of milk'.
2 Your grandchild then says, 'I went to market and I bought a bottle of milk, and an apple'.
3 Then it's your turn, 'I went to market and I bought a bottle of milk, an apple and a loaf of bread'. And the game continues in this way.

This is a good game because there is no 'winner' – you help each other remember by prompting or having real food or objects as reminders. You can draw pictures or write a list for reference if necessary. Having these reminders isn't cheating and this game can help develop memory skills.

The alphabet game

Resources:

- pen
- paper
- or plastic alphabet letters.

This game has always been a favourite in our family, especially on long car journeys or wet Sunday afternoons. Any number of people can play but make sure a different person starts each time or you will each always get the same letters.

1 You can either write the alphabet on a piece of paper or put plastic letters into alphabetical order. For young children leave out the harder letters such as X and Z.
2 You then suggest a category, for example, animals' or girls' names.
3 You then take a letter each and say an animal or name starting with that letter or sound.

This game helps children think and learn about sounds and about categories, e.g. animals, foods, etc.

Simon says

Another no-resource game that children always enjoy. You and your grandchild can take it turns to be the leader (and a few mistakes from you will boost his/her self-esteem no end!).

1 Give your grandchild a series of instructions such as 'Simon says stand up', 'Simon says touch your nose', 'Simon says...' etc.
2 After a few 'Simon says' give an instruction without 'Simon says', for example 'Turn around'. If your grandchild does turn around then their turn ends and they take over the lead – now it's your turn.

This game is good for concentration and listening because you only do what *Simon* says – nothing else.

Sock sort

Resources:

- a bag
- 21 socks – ten pairs and one odd one.

Another simple but effective game that children love – and a good way of sorting out your sock drawer!

1 Put all the socks into the bag and take it in turns to pull one out – without looking.
2 Talk about each sock, its colour, pattern, who it might have belonged to…etc. If you can make a pair of socks put them together.
3 The winner is the person with five pairs and no odd sock out.

Modelling listening skills

Parents of young children frequently complain that their child is not listening to them; teenagers frequently complain that their *parents* do not listen to *them*. Listening is a common breakdown in families and a source of frustration. Grandparents are often well placed to model good listening behaviours.

Pitfalls

First let us look at some of the listening 'sins' that we are all guilty of at times.

- Questions and Advice: When children have a series of questions adults can be quick to give out advice, although they have not fully understood the issue.
- Pretend Listening: We half-listen, nod and make encouraging noises whilst working out what time to put the potatoes on.
- Selective Listening: We have already decided what the child is going to say or we only want to hear one message and we listen out for things that confirm our view or prejudices.
- Self-centred Listening: We interpret what is being said from our own perspective and this can lead to us asking probing questions in order to make judgements. Or we are listening in order to bring the topic back to talking about ourselves.
- Word Listening: This is a close cousin of 'pretend listening' and often happens when we are listening whilst busy doing something else. We hear the words the child uses but do not

observe their body language. This leads to misunderstanding the child, especially their emotions and feelings.

- Breaking Confidences: We encourage the child to tell us something, but do not first make it clear if we will hold the confidence or need to tell another person (such as the other parent).
- False Reassurances and Breaking Promises: We can listen to a child and over-empathize and want to rescue them with reassurances and promises to make them happy and solve their problems. In our haste these badly-thought-out promises and reassurances cannot be kept and trust is lost.

Successes

When we avoid these pitfalls we are perceived by our children as genuine and sincere listeners. Some of the key things to remember are:

- Observe your grandchild's body language; it may give you a more accurate idea about how they are feeling than their words.
- First try to listen with an open mind so that you can see the world through their eyes.
- Acknowledge and validate their thoughts and feelings.
- Make their efforts to communicate with you rewarding and enjoyable so that they will want to talk to you more often.

Of course demonstrating good listening skills when a child is younger makes a grandparent more approachable during the teenage years and into adulthood – vital when we consider how many teenagers accuse their parents of just not listening!

Communicating with children

Parents can find communicating with their children difficult. The following points can help:

- Put yourself in their shoes.
- Listen with an open mind.
- Allow plenty of time for the child to talk and explain.
- Ask open questions designed to help your understanding.
- Acknowledge and validate the feelings they express.

The aim is to see the situation from the child's perspective so that you can understand how they are experiencing life and what they feel about it. To do this properly means putting yourself, your experiences and judgements to one side. Parents and grandparents often try to think back to when they were that age to help them understand; but this can lead to interpreting what the child is saying to them through their own eyes. It's worth reminding yourself that everyone's experience is unique and that times have changed; teenagers face different challenges today.

Teenagers often confide in grandparents more than parents. Listening on a regular basis, in order to understand your grandchild's life, will mean that you are likely to be more aware of the small, everyday issues going on; these may seem trivial to you, but your level of awareness will tune you in to the kinds of things that concern young people. Frequent conversations will also heighten your awareness of your grandchild's body language to help you gauge when to pick a good moment for a talk and when to back off.

When grandchildren are young, listen to the problem and tell them what to do. As they grow older, try to encourage self-reliance by fading out direct advice-giving and instead help them to work through the problem, providing suggestions but ultimately leaving them to formulate an action plan.

What if a child has difficulty communicating?

Grandparents are often the first to notice a child having problems with speaking, listening and communicating.

Over 1 million children in the UK have some kind of communication disability.

Children with communication difficulties might:

- have difficulties with speech sounds
- find it hard to understand language (receptive skills)
- find it hard to produce language (expressive skills)
- have difficulties with using language appropriately in context (social skills).

There are many ways to describe the difficulties a child or young person may be having with communication. These depend on a whole range of factors, including:

- which areas of language they are having difficulty with
- how severely affected these areas are
- what skills and strengths the child or young person has
- how they need to use their language – e.g. at school
- their confidence and self-esteem.

If you are concerned you and the child's parents can do a number of things to help. You can contact your local speech and language therapy department and ask for an appointment. Your grandchild's GP or Health Visitor will do this for you if you ask them. There is often a waiting list for speech and language therapy appointments. This may be due to a large number of children needing appointments. In many areas there is a shortage of speech and language therapists.

For more information, you could contact Afasic. They have a helpline where you can get detailed information. It is open Monday to Friday from 10.30 a.m. until 2.30 p.m. The number is 0845 355 5577. See **www.afasic.org.uk**. I CAN also host the talking point information service: **www.talkingpoint.org.uk**.

Getting advice from professionals may:

- reassure you if your grandchild has minor difficulties that can be helped easily, or if your grandchild's communication development is fine
- give you more ideas of ways to help your grandchild's communication development
- lead to the right kind of help, if your grandchild is having particular difficulties with their communication.

However, waiting for appointments can sometimes be frustrating and add to your concerns.

Here are some ideas to help in the meantime:

- Make a note of the sorts of things your grandchild is having difficulty with. This can provide useful information when your grandchild does get an appointment. Noting examples of what your grandchild says or doesn't say can be really helpful.
- Help your grandchild to develop and maintain their confidence. Even if a child is having some difficulties, there will be numerous things they are very good at. Supporting their attempts and celebrating their successes can help a child or young person regain confidence.

- The I CAN website (**www.ican.org.uk/families**) has lots of information for parents and grandparents as well as the opportunity to order free DVD's and packs including Chatter Matters and Ready, Steady Talk.
- Finally, try to encourage discussion with your grandchild's pre-school or school teacher to gain a full picture of their difficulties.

Checklist

1 Take an interest in your grandchild's school.
2 Try to attend school events if possible.
3 Talk to the teachers if you drop children off or pick them up from school.
4 Talk with your grandchildren as it is a key way they develop language skills.
5 Play simple games to teach memory, maths and language skills.
6 Try to develop your own listening skills with your grandchildren.

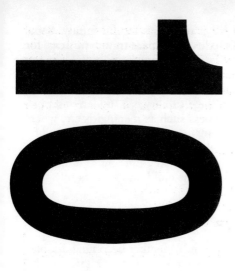

10

disability within the family

In this chapter you will learn:
- how to cope with your feelings about disability
- how disability affects other family members
- how you can help with care and support.

Nobody is ever prepared for a disability in the family. Some children are born with a disability and this is traumatic news for everyone at that time. However, with support, most children can experience a good quality of life. In this chapter Paul Smith, Chief Executive of Spinal Injuries Association, advises on how grandparents can cope when the disability is a sudden onset one i.e. through an accident, or illness such as meningitis etc. where a healthy child is suddenly transformed into one requiring life-changing adjustments. The feelings and issues discussed here are relevant for all families with a disabled child and grandparents can be a great help in the life of the child and their family.

Hearing the news

No one can be prepared for a family member becoming disabled through conditions such as a spinal cord injury (SCI) – this includes the newly-injured individual and those around them such as family and friends. If you are one of those that experiences the trauma of a sudden onset disability for your grandchild you will keep forever vivid recollections of when you were told and how and the intense emotion that you felt. There is no easy way to tell someone that their grandchild will be paralyzed for the rest of their life and unfortunately, for some, the fact may be reported to them in an insensitive and unsatisfactory manner.

The emotional feelings that need to be tackled are not just restricted to the child, the whole family will have issues to deal with, particularly the parents, siblings and grandparents. In many cases, there can be a feeling of guilt generated by a belief that they should have been able to keep the child safe from harm. These feelings are generally misguided as in most circumstances the accident or situation that results in the injury may not have been preventable.

We all react differently to bad news and in the case of a SCI, which is seen as devastating, reactions can vary widely, the first reaction is usually one of shock. This can manifest itself in many forms from bursting into tears to what could be perceived as switching off. Grief is a common emotion that those surrounding the child will face. The period following the sudden onset of disability is often referred to as bereavement and the grief experienced can be equal to that if the child had died. Like bereavement, those affected can take differing lengths of time to accept what has happened. Grief can, in some instances, lead to feelings of despair which when dwelled upon can spiral out of control creating ever-increasing depression and sadness. People experiencing this need a lot of support and if this affects the parents the grandparents have a major role to play in helping them through it and helping to mask it from the child.

That is not to say that everyone experiences all or any of the above feelings. There will always be positive people who rise to the challenge but those around them may not understand. This reaction should not be confused with denial, which is the hardest reaction for those around an individual to deal with because it can hinder rehabilitation of the child and the adaptation that will be needed for life to continue. It is at this point that grandparents can sometimes take on the role of counsellor to help to support the family.

It is important to be honest with yourself. It is not wrong to feel negative emotions as they are normal but many people try to hide them because they believe that they need to be strong. Parents often struggle with this and can falter without support. Who better to provide this than their own parents. The challenge is knowing when to step back and when to come forward. Sometimes there can be a temptation when they see their child failing to cope to try and take over – this sometimes is not good for their children or the injured grandchild.

Early stages

In the early stages after injury there is often mention of 'coping' with the traumatic change. 'Coping' is used to describe a wide range of responses that are used by all concerned with the newly-injured person. Many of the coping strategies used by the grandparents will revolve around emotion-focused coping in which they will attempt to control the emotions they are experiencing in coming to terms with their situation.

In addition, there will also be the need for problem-focused coping to tackle the practical problems which arise from the change in circumstances. It is often difficult for parents to look at the practical issues as the emotions can overtake them. This is where the grandparents can play an important role.

It is important in the early days that follow a severe injury or illness that grandparents do not allow the worry to have either a physical or psychological impact on their own health. They should talk openly about what has happened but not try to apportion blame (what is done is done and there is no going back – they must look to the future). It will be important to keep conflict to a minimum. They will need to maintain as positive a frame of mind as they can for the sake of their grandchild and the others in the family and, above all, keep hold of the ability to laugh. They will need to be positive and not dwell on what may not now be possible. In today's society a disabled child can grow up to live a full and rewarding life with the same aspirations as those without a disability.

Treatment and rehabilitation

There is a big debate amongst the medical profession as to where it is best for newly-disabled children with conditions such as a spinal cord injury to go for their acute treatment and rehabilitation. Up until recently the only option was for the child to go to a specialist spinal cord injuries centre where they would likely be the only child on a ward of adults – which can be a frightening experience. There is also the fact that the nurses working in the specialist centres may not have received the appropriate level of training to deal with the particular needs of children. The other option is for the newly-injured child to be treated and cared for on a paediatric ward where the nursing staff know all about the needs of children but will not have the specialist knowledge to best treat the spinal cord injury. This is the first of many quandaries facing the immediate family of a newly-injured child. Thankfully specialist paediatric wards are starting to be established in specialist spinal cord injury centres but these are few and far between and the likelihood of one being near where the child lives is rare. Therefore, there may be another decision to make, whether it is better to get the child to a specialist centre or to local services where family support is close to hand?

The challenge for the family of a disabled child is to provide an environment in which the child can develop both psychologically and physically. It is important not just to focus on the physical issues – often the greatest hurdles that need to be overcome are the emotional ones.

One of the most important things a grandparent can do in the early stages that follow any disability or severe illness is to gain a good understanding of what it is and the mechanics of the condition or illness – in particular, the care needs that may arise. There are lots of publications on the subjects and many specific advice lines which provide support and information.

Impact on the family

Stress within the family increases greatly when such an episode of injury or illness occurs but despite this fact it is believed that families are more likely to stay together after a spinal cord injury, because of the need to pull together for the good of the injured child. Sadly, statistics relating to all disabilities show that for some families the stress is too great and the children may also experience the breakdown of the relationship between their parents. Grandparents can play a big part in keeping the stresses at bay by providing support for the parents.

Having a child with a disability will inevitably refocus a parent's attention on their newborn, newly-injured or disabled child – this can be at the expense of their brothers and sisters. If parents are not careful siblings can feel left out, in particular if they are very young.

Impact on siblings

It is fairly easy for an adult to work out that if one child needs more time spent with them then the remaining children in the family will have reduced time and attention spent on them. It can be hard to understand that they do not love one child more than another and that it is just a case that the sick or disabled brother/sister may need individual attention to carry out basic functions. Having a brother or sister with a disability can affect a child's psychological development, which can appear in a number of ways including being aggressive towards members of their family. They may also develop a fear that they could develop the same condition.

Grandparents can play a major role in their grandchildren's adjustment to the altered circumstance of their sibling. This may involve trying to encourage the other children to support their brother/sister – by being involved they can feel a part of something that they may perceive is taking over their family and home.

Grandparents should be aware that the grandchildren will react differently to their sibling at this time. The age of the child will be a big factor – a young child is unlikely to fully understand what is going on. Also, the level and severity of injury or illness will also impact on their adjustment. When discussing with young children the injury or illness and the impact it has had on the newly disabled child, it is important to talk in such a way that they understand and are not scared.

It should also be considered that having a disabled brother or sister can have some positive influences on the child's psychological development. Siblings often develop strong compassionate characteristics and have increased levels of tolerance. It has even been said that they develop greater self-confidence.

The disabled/injured child

It is all too easy to fall into the trap of wrapping the newly-injured child in cotton wool and being over-protective. Many grandparents believe it is their right to over-indulge their grandchildren but this over-indulgence can also be joined by the desire to protect them from harm – particularly in the case of a child whose injury has come about as a result of an accident. These two actions can result in the extended dependency of the disabled child, which is not good for their development as adults.

The child may not want their parents or grandparents to be their constant support. It can be hard for a family to bring in carers/personal assistants from outside the circle of family and friends to help the child to have independence. For many the idea of them moving away from home seems impossible as the family and their friends believe they will always need to be there to provide care for the child. This only stores up problems for the future when the family carers are no longer able to provide the support.

Care needs and support

Some grandparents try to involve themselves in the care the child needs when they return home. While this may be well intentioned it could cause problems if the child or their parents do not welcome it. Good communication skills are vital in this area and listening skills play a crucial part of this. Just because the child accepts an offer of help may not necessarily mean that they want it – it may be accepted to help the person who offered. In some cases the newly-injured child can feel guilty and feel that their actions have caused difficulties for the family and so they become submissive, not wishing to cause trouble. It's important to aim for as much independence as possible for the child without being harsh.

When the child is in hospital the level of support that can be offered to the child by the grandparent will be limited. It is when they go home and start to live the rest of their lives that the support grandparents can give moves from emotional support to a more practical level. It is fairly self explanatory that the sick or disabled child may need extra care from parents and the support of grandparents can play an important part in reducing the pressure that comes about through meeting these extra needs.

It is important for a child with restricted mobility to avoid getting a pressure sore – damaging skin at an early age can have a major impact on the rest of their life. For this reason, it's important that good pressure care is maintained which may mean that parents have to get up several times during the night to turn the child to ensure pressure sores do not occur. They may also need to provide assistance with getting dressed and undressed. A particular concern to both the child and those providing care support will be the issues around bladder and bowel management. This will have come as a bit of a shock for most people – the average person can relate to the need to use a wheelchair but will not have thought about the hidden problems that come with a disability. Some of the things that a parent or primary carer has to do, such as catheterization, can be hard to come to terms with and may almost seem like an assault on the child. One of the biggest challenges a parent and grandparent may face will be if the child sustains a high-level neck injury that means the child has to be dependant on a ventilator to breathe.

It will be important for the family to return to a normal pattern of social life to relieve the stresses and strains. The grandparent caring for the child and providing activities can provide the parents with a much-needed respite. However, it is worth bearing in mind that whilst there are support networks for SCI people (including children) and to a certain extent they are there for parents and husbands and wives as well, albeit informal, there is not really anything for grandparents who share in many of the emotional issues that parents do. Likewise, when it comes to the initial stages of acute treatment they tend to receive their information through third parties; and being outside the decision-making process grandparents often feel powerless and are left feeling frustrated.

Discipline

Grandparents might also find discipline difficult to maintain. It can be hard to discipline a child with a disability as you may feel that you are being harsh and unsympathetic to the problems the child is facing. Becoming disabled or ill does not make the child into an angel and may in fact prompt them to push their luck and extend the boundaries that form normal standards.

The problem comes when the rules are broken and you have to discipline the child. You must be prepared to show them the consequences of their actions; empty threats will just teach the child that their grandparents are a pushover and they can get away with doing whatever they want. Whatever the consequence, this should be talked through with the parents as a consistent message is important. It is also important that the consequence fits the behaviour and is of the same level as would be given to the non-disabled siblings. Failure to promote good behaviour from a child is a form of over-indulgence.

Understanding and adapting

Children with a spinal cord injury will essentially have the same needs as an adult with this type of injury. They will also have additional needs however as the very young will not fully understand what has happened and why certain procedures need to be done. It is hard for adults to comprehend the changes in their bodies but for a child who has no understanding of how their body functions it can be a frightening experience. It is not just a case of not being able to move certain limbs – those who suffer from spasms have to learn to accept that their muscles and limbs may move independently, some just in the form of a twitch and for others so severe that they can be thrown out of a chair or bed.

When the initial rehabilitation has finished it's important to ensure that the newly-injured child does not feel socially isolated – this can be difficult to achieve and a lot depends on the social networks they had before their injury. It can be exceedingly frustrating for a grandparent to see a child looking isolated and the temptation is to try and replace the child's normal circle of friends through greater involvement. While this may seem a good idea at the time it could lead to problems later when the child gets older and needs to develop their network of friends – in particular, if they want to go away to university. Both the parents and grandparents should pull together in a strategy that develops the child's self-confidence. The SCI child may try to avoid contact that is not seen as necessary but you should teach them ways of making the first move and engaging with their peers. It's important to give them lots of social experiences by inviting children of their own age to play – but make sure you anticipate the behaviour of those new friends and try to explain the differences that may crop up when they talk.

Hopes and aspirations

Like parents – grandparents will have built up aspirations for their grandchild and at first it will seem that these have been dashed forever. It's important not to create a 'self-fulfilling' prophecy. Just because the grandchild has an illness or disability it does not mean that they will achieve any less than they would have if the accident/experience had not happened. There is no reason why they cannot achieve academic excellence, have a good job, get married, and nowadays even have children of their own. Anything is possible with the right motivation but if the grandparents are negative the child is likely to feed off this and believe they should have reduced expectations. Obviously these have to be realistic – it is unlikely that a SCI child will grow up to be a jet fighter pilot but with the right support they may be able to achieve something equally as exciting and as demanding but within their physical abilities. Having said that, one of the most well known World War II pilots was Douglas Bader who flew after having both his legs amputated.

Grandparents to a child with a disability

We are a family with three boys, one who is five years old and twins who are six. Five years ago our lives were changed completely when one of our sons contracted meningitis. Over a period of four months he was in and out of various hospitals while he was seriously ill. At last he came home, but his illness had left him profoundly deaf.

Grandparents on both sides of the family played an important role both during the initial crisis period, and in the years afterwards. We have all learned in our various ways to cope with what has happened.

Our family was living overseas when Matthew became sick. Matthew's grandmother, my mother, flew out and arrived that evening; for my husband and myself knowing that someone we loved and trusted was in there house looking after the other children was invaluable. During those first two desperate weeks as our son lay in a coma in intensive care, my mother managed to support us in our emotions, without ever once displaying her own. She kept her grief inside, and only talked about it when, months later, I brought the subject up. She gave me the time to be totally emotionally selfish, knowing more than I did that this was all I could manage.

On my husband's side, the grandparents gave us generous physical support; they opened their house to us and fed us. But they were not able to give the emotional support that my mother had done. There was a lack of that deep understanding of what we had all been through and what we all needed. Their emotional needs were high, and I was stretched to meet them. At the time, that hurt. Looking back, I realize that they gave what they could.

In the years that followed, our son has received two cochlear implants. We decided to follow the aural/oral route and not use sign language. He is now a talking child, attending a mainstream school and doing well. He will always be deaf and have to overcome serious obstacles, but to our family he is a normal, happy, little boy.

Grandparents and family members have been wonderful and supportive. But almost more important has been the unquestioning support from my mother in our choices for our son. Grandparents have the ability to look back at their lives and realize the truly important things in life with a clarity that those of us in the middle of it rarely possess. We wanted to do everything in our power to enable him reach his full potential, and it was rewarding that we could rely on my mother to appreciate all his achievements.

As a disabled child he has been totally accepted and not spoiled. All his grandparents thoroughly enjoy his company but they have also given more time to our other children. Lengthy periods in hospital, and frequent operations meant that much attention was focused on our deaf son. Both sets of grandparents helped redress the balance, and often gave the other children emotional support that as parents we were too 'caught up in it all' to do. They also at times pointed this out to us – not appreciated at the time but probably a good thing in the long run.

Checklist

1 Get more information on the disability from hospitals and self-help groups.
2 Give extra help by doing more to look after siblings.
3 Learn about the special needs a disabled child may have when caring for them.
4 Try to help the family return to a normal pattern of social life.
5 Help make sure the disabled child is not socially isolated.
6 Try and provide emotional support for the parents.
7 Don't hide your own negative emotions.
8 Don't take over completely from the parents.

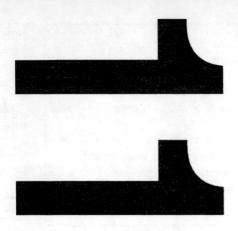

in times
of trouble

In this chapter you will learn:
- how to cope if you become the sole carer
- what to do in the case of separation/divorce
- what to do if children have suffered harm.

Things can go wrong in any family whatever the circumstances and in any event nearly all families go through a 'bad patch' from time to time. Grandparents and other family members usually rally round to help in such an unobtrusive way that an outside observer would not be aware that anything had gone wrong. The range of help that is given is large, but childcare, financial help, engaging practical help from outside agencies, or just general support and advice are a few examples that readily spring to mind.

Sadly, more serious incidents can have a greater significance and longer lasting impact on children. Accidents or illness can afflict a happy, thriving family, just as family breakdown splits less happy families apart. Children can suffer harm because their parents are unable or unwilling to care for them. In all these situations grandparents may or may not play a vital role. Some grandparents take on a major role in caring for their grandchildren, others may not be able to do so nor wish to, while yet others may wish to be involved but find they are prevented from doing so in some way.

Natural tragedy

A fatal accident or illness can leave a child without one or both their parents. Grandparents often step into the breach to look after their grandchildren full time, part time or in a supporting capacity.

If grandparents have sole care of their grandchildren they do not automatically have parental responsibility for the children and there are usually all sorts of other legal and financial matters that require guidance. Most of these issues can be resolved but it is essential that the caring grandparents seek legal advice. Financial matters, however small and insignificant they may seem, should be sorted out.

Get legal advice before going to court

You will need to take legal advice to establish whether a court can make orders to secure the future legal status and residence for the children which may be particularly important if, for example, the situation is not made clear in the parents' will. The courts can usually resolve your legal status so that the grandparent can take important decisions about their grandchildren such as decisions regarding hospital treatment.

It may also make decisions in favour of the grandparent which states that the child will live with the grandparent until they reach the age of 18 years.

Parental separation

Parental breakdown and separation are extremely difficult and traumatic situations for the children to handle and some may be affected for a long time – even for years to come. Children caught up in these situations are always sad, upset and insecure. This can show itself in many different ways and at any age. Their behaviour can alter inexplicably; their work at school can suffer; and their relationships with their peers may change. Children often feel guilty thinking that they are in some way to blame for the break-up. They are often caught up in the crossfire between the parents and may takes sides with one parent against the other.

The situation can be equally tricky for grandparents, especially if they are also somehow caught up in the disagreement between the parents. Grandparents who enjoy a close relationship with their grandchildren however can be a rock to them in times of trouble, and can support and help them through difficult times.

Most families sort out the problems of separation amicably and in the best interest of the children, who remain on good terms with each side of the family. They are able to maintain contact with each parent, grandparents, and cousins by agreement between them. Grandparents usually help where they can and continue to have a good relationship with their grandchildren.

Going to court

However, in a small but significant number of families, grandparents are in danger of losing contact with their grandchildren, especially if the relationship between the parents is acrimonious and their son or daughter becomes the non-resident parent or the parent without care. If the grandparents want contact with their grandchildren and it is being prevented they may be able to go to a court to ask for an order enabling them to have contact or visitation rights. In the US this will be dependent on State Law, The AARP Grandparents Information Center publishes leaflets giving guidance on the law for each State relating to visitation rights.

AARP Grandparents need to think long and hard before taking any legal action, as it will involve the whole family and they will have to show that contact visits are in the best interests of the child before a court may intervene. It is essential that legal advice is taken before embarking on this route. If grandparents do not have direct contact with their grandchildren they can try to maintain indirect contact by sending cards and gifts at birthdays and Christmas. The Grandparents' Association in the UK can give initial advice and put grandparents in touch with a solicitor in order to obtain legal advice.

Children who have suffered harm

There are a small but significant number of children who have suffered or who are at risk of suffering harm and the State or Childcare Protection Agency will intervene to protect them. This harm can be neglect, emotional harm, physical harm or sexual abuse. If nothing is done by the parents to stop the harm or potential harm and they do not cooperate with social workers, legal proceedings will commence to remove the children from the home and take them into a safe environment such as foster care.

The following list includes a few examples that could be viewed as harm. A child could be said to suffer significant harm if:

- they have witnessed domestic violence between their parents
- they sustain a non-accidental injury
- they have been physically assaulted
- they are neglected perhaps due to drug and alcohol abuse of the parents
- they disclose to someone that they have been sexually assaulted
- they are kept at home for long periods to care for a sick relative, thereby becoming isolated.

Grandparents may be among the first to recognize if a grandchild is exposed to risk and detect early signs of change in the demeanour or behaviour of the child. They should take steps to protect the child as far as they are able by working with the unabusive parent to prevent the child suffering harm. This could be practical help to relieve pressure, or discussing behaviour change and possible solutions with the unabusive parent. If the situation deteriorates, or if both parents are abusive, grandparents should approach a Child Protection Agency or Local Authority for assistance as the welfare of the child is paramount.

Many grandparents step in and take care of the grandchildren on a voluntary basis and appear to do a good enough job. When the Child Protection Agency or Local Authority intervenes however, the situation may well change. Under legislation the Local Authority or Childcare Protection Team have a duty to consider placing a child with members of the extended family if at all possible and will carry out an independent assessment of the grandparent as a suitable carer.

Grandparents sometimes find this difficult to understand as they may well be already caring for the child, but the Local Authority or Childcare Protection Agency will need to assess them as if they are potential foster parents before officially placing the child with them. Assessments are very thorough and this means that several different social workers will probably be visiting and asking searching questions. They will also be examining the relationship between the parents and the grandparent to ensure that if the grandparent is to be the carer they can protect the child from harm.

At this stage the situation can become confusing for the grandparent. A grandmother who wishes to care for her grandchild is sometimes found not to be suitable, and another grandmother who feels she cannot take on that role especially if there are one or more siblings to be placed for example, may be put under pressure to take on the role of carer. The grandparent should remain calm and seek both legal advice and advice from Social Services. If the child is placed outside the family the grandparent may wish to discuss contact and visitation rights with a social worker.

If the grandparent is considered the best carer for the child, it's important to recognize that legal advice is necessary, not only to decide whether or not the grandparent should become involved in legal proceedings but to help the grandparent understand what is in the best interests of the child.

The role of the grandparent

During times of trouble, it's important to remember that the focal point is always what is in the best interests of the child. With so many other things going on it's easy to forget this, but grandparents are more detached and therefore ideally placed to help protect the children. Children, whatever their age, need nurture, stability, security and a framework for development, and of course love.

The better the relationship grandparents have with their grandchildren the more they are able to help. They too can bond with babies or just be there for the older children and it's important to remember to ask them what they would like to happen. Children often complain that when everybody is deciding what is best for them no one asks them.

Although times of trouble can be traumatic for children, it's worth remembering that many of them are very resilient and what they need most of all is to know that someone is there for them and cares what happens to them.

Checklist

1 Grandparents who look after their grandchildren full-time do not automatically have parental responsibility for them.

2 Make sure you get legal advice before going to court in any custody hearings.

3 In the case of separation or divorce, try and maintain contact with grandchildren – by cards and gifts if not by direct visits.

4 Think hard before going to court to gain visitation rights, as the legal battle could involve the whole family.

5 Be alert to possible signs of child harm or abuse, such as non-accidental injuries, assault, or neglect.

6 Try and protect the child by working with the other parent.

7 Contact a child protection agency or local authority if the situation persists.

8 Consider taking a caring role if the parents are judged unsuitable – but be aware that this will involve an assessment by the local authority.

12

stepchildren in the family

In this chapter you will learn:
- the different ways you can become a step-grandparent
- why names are such an emotional issue
- how to think about your role.

Families are often a lot more complicated nowadays and research shows that 20 per cent of the under 70s in the UK are step-grandparents. This was fairly common over 100 years ago when many parents died tragically young, as those of us researching family history can attest, but today many of us acknowledge the different roles within the family.

Becoming a step-grandparent

There are many ways to become a step-grandparent and it is different for us all. It may be that your partner becomes a grandparent when a child from an earlier relationship gives birth. Indeed, I know many step-grandparents in this situation who have never been parents themselves and becoming a step-grandparent is their first experience of playing a major role in such a young child's life.

However, the birth of the baby may lead to some very complicated feelings within the family. Sometimes the new step-grandparent may feel resentful. If there is a significant age difference they may not like the idea of becoming a grandparent or being the partner of one. Usually all eyes are on the baby and the new parents but this can lead to some feelings of either jealousy or resentment. Perhaps the birth will bring your partner into contact with their 'ex' again, the children from that relationship become the centre of their attention and maybe you will feel that this is all focusing on a time in their life when you were not a part of it or it stirs up feelings from an earlier time. If you have children between you there may be an element of believing that your partner is favouring the older child. This is perfectly normal but so is the wish to be involved when that baby is born and all parties may need to understand this.

Henry and Suzette's story

Henry and Suzette were less than enthusiastic about being step-grandparents and still strenuously deny that they are grandparents at all. They have a daughter, Alison, who married a father of two, but the boys live with their mother and so it has been easy for them to distance themselves from the children as they only stay with their father and stepmother once a month.

They also failed to acknowledge that when Alison and Jeff married she became the children's stepmother. Alison finds it hard to manage her role as stepparent and would have welcomed more support from her parents in her maternal role.

Mike and Diane's story

Mike and Diane are grandparents of a young boy. After their son and his partner split up the boy's mother met and married someone else and went on to have two more children. All three children regard them as their grandparents and all three stay at the house and spend time with them. Mike and Diane have put the best interests of all the children first and not their own feelings about what happened between the adults. They are rewarded by knowing they have helped their grandson to adjust to his life with his stepfather and younger siblings.

What's in a name?

So what does a step-grandchild call you? If they are young you can pretty much guarantee that they will come up with a name themselves that you had never thought of!

Jack's story

Jack is three years old and he calls his maternal grandmother 'red door nanny' a name that he came up with at about the age of two to differentiate between his two sets of grandparents. His step-grandparents are 'nanny and grandad' (and he hates it when only one of them is around) and his great-grandmother is 'stairs nanny'.

The key here is to be led by the children and the sensitivities of those around you.

In all the chapters in this book we are constantly stating that the child comes first. We know what children mean to us and whether you are known as Susan, auntie Susan or nanny doesn't really matter. Usually, it's the adults that cause conflict rather than children and using a name to signify that one person has a better relationship with the child may be damaging to the whole family relationship.

Just be proud that you have the children in the family and enjoy their young lives – they grow up far too fast and we never get that time back.

Raymond and Roberta's story

Raymond and Roberta became step-grandparents when their son, Justin, married somebody with three children. They found it very strange for the first few months of Justin's relationship as they were usually very open and welcoming towards their son's new girlfriends. As this relationship began, Roberta knew she and Raymond were being more cautious in accepting Suzie into the family.

They were afraid that lavishing too much love and attention on Suzie's very young children during the early stages of the relationship could be harmful to the children. Roberta and Raymond worried that if the relationship went no further the children would, in fact, miss their contact and love too. They held back until they and the children could be confident the relationship would last.

Roberta and Raymond have found that the circumstances of becoming step-grandparents altered how they felt about their role. They treat the children in exactly the same way as they treat their birth grandchildren. Perhaps this is because, in their case, the children live with their mother and after they got married their son became a 'resident parent'. This meant that any outings, holidays, visits etc. automatically included the children.

When the step-grandchildren first became part of their lives they called Raymond and Roberta by their first names. But, after a couple of years, the middle son asked if he could call them nanny and grandad. Raymond and Roberta were more than happy with this but they did ask his maternal grandmother for her views – she was delighted. Their daughter-in-law was also happy in the arrangement as she encouraged the idea that there were more people interested in the lives of her children. The older and younger brother initially decided that they would continue to call them by their first names but, within the month, they started to use nanny and grandad too, and this remains so today.

Joy's story

I first met my step-grandchildren when the girl was six years old and the boy three, and they were in the process of recovering from the unhappy and much-fought-over divorce of their parents. Subsequently, my son married their mother and within three months the law separated the siblings. The girl was ordered to go to her father in Scotland and the boy to his mother and stepfather in Africa.

For the last 17 years they have travelled backwards and forwards from Africa to Scotland and vice versa, each of them for two holidays in the year. I have been privileged to meet them countless times at Heathrow airport while changing flights. Nearly always there was a two or three hour gap between planes during which we would visit the restaurant and have time for a real talk and catch-up on news. It amazes me how well I know them. Possibly because we are not directly related, our meetings are relaxed and we all really enjoy holiday time together, whether in Africa or, more recently, when they have stayed with me in England.

Checklist

1 Remember that one in five grandparents are step-grandparents.

2 Be sensitive to what name your step-grandchildren call you.

3 Be proud of all the children in your family.

4 Avoid feelings of favouritism concerning the children of your partner.

5 Make sure that the emotional needs of partners are not neglected.

6 Get support when difficult feelings about past relationships are stirred up.

13

maintaining visits to grandchildren

In this chapter you will learn:
- how to keep in touch with older grandchildren
- how to cope with different expectations about family events
- maintaining contact after divorce/separation
- how to seek help when there has been family conflict.

Most grandparents will see their grandchildren on a regular basis and continue to have visits agreed by the parents until they reach adulthood. Older children are likely to reach a stage when extra curricular activities and active social lives mean they see family less often. This is to be encouraged and grandparents may become cheerleaders for their activities – on the sports field, on stage or at the local pool. Even if you can't be there in person, having an active and shared interest may help keep lines of communication open. Keeping in contact can include using email and mobile phones – more favoured by teenagers than traditional letter writing.

May's story

May was a widow whose daughter, Leila, lived a very busy work life and was a mature student. As a result, May rarely saw her only granddaughter Anna. When Anna was eight years old she was the star of her school play on the very day that her mother had to take her qualifying examinations. May was pleased when Leila reluctantly asked her mother to go along in her place. May also offered to help with costumes to give her daughter more time to revise.

Leila had been avoiding seeing her mother or asking for help because she was afraid her mother was still disapproving of her divorce four years earlier. May was able to reassure her daughter that she had long since got over her initial shock of the divorce and whilst she was proud of her daughter's independence she would be happy to help any time. She told Leila she very much regretted being so angry at the time of the divorce and not apologizing earlier.

Sharing time

- It's not unusual for families to be vague as to their expectations as to how often they will be in touch and/or see each other. Your expectations may be very different from your son or daughter's partner; you may feel hurt if the only contact you have is when you are asked to babysit.
- Misunderstandings can arise around celebrations of birthdays and other family occasions.
- A good way forward is to develop a good understanding of your role in family life, balancing your needs with those of your family.

- Perhaps you might like to suggest a diary planning session every few months that could include some family treats and activities that every generation could enjoy.
- Some families holiday together, including uncles, aunts and cousins, and enjoy trawling through the possibilities of family journeys.
- Others prefer movies, concerts, or theatre matinees for shows that all the family can enjoy, or sporting events, meeting up for picnics or Sunday brunch.
- Concentrate on having lots of fun and letting people have space to enjoy each other's company.

Holiday time

- If your family are not going to see you on key festivals (Christmas, Thanksgiving, New Year etc.), take time to find others who might like to share a meal with you or volunteer to help out in a local charity or hospital.
- Alternatively, choose this time to holiday with a friend or partner.
- Try to have a willing acceptance that once your children have their own families they may sometimes have conflicting demands. Support them to juggle the many responsibilities they have.
- Ask well in advance about the plans of your family and don't assume they will always make the same choices.
- Some grandparents may prefer to schedule family time when travel costs are lower and expectations can be more easily managed.

Balance your life

Changes in your own life may mean you may become increasingly dependant on your family for company. This can put pressure on relationships, particularly if you are feeling lonely and depressed when they are not around. It can be helpful for you and your family to know you have your own life and activities demanding your time. Take time to enjoy your free time; if this feels too difficult you may like to discuss your situation with a doctor or counsellor rather than blame your loneliness on your children.

Relationship breakdown

One common trigger for losing contact with grandchildren is the difficulty of maintaining contact during and after the breakdown of the relationship between the grandchild's parents or step-parents.

Grandparents may want to intervene and find it almost unbearable to see their family in pain and want to provide help and assistance. Tell everyone in your family that you have a wish to do everything you can to support your grandchildren. Young children are frequently confused when the people they care about most part company. At this time the adults are often unable to find the time and energy to fully focus on the needs of the children. Grandparents can have an important role in the lives of their grandchildren when their lives seem upside down. Children benefit from reassurance at times of change – that they are loved, that it is not their fault and that they have someone to talk to about their feelings. It's important to remember they may feel conflicting loyalties – listening without criticizing either parent will help them continue to talk about their feelings. Children may feel they are to blame for adult disagreements – a grandparent is often well placed to help children understand the changes in their life are not their fault.

Some grandparents may feel that their adult child should have behaved differently, particularly if there is a third party involved. Hold back on criticism and see the parting of a child's parents as a difficult time for all concerned.

Maintaining contact

The choices your son or daughter will be making are theirs alone to make at this stage and attempts to engineer either a reconciliation or withdrawal of all contact with their former or new partner may damage your chance of retaining contact with the grandchildren. In the meantime, your grandchildren will benefit from your support for them to continue to have a relationship with both their parents and their wider family. Acknowledging and accepting the changes in the family life and negotiating with all concerned how this will affect their contact with you will help you to maintain and continue contact.

You may want to communicate with the former partner to negotiate when you see your grandchildren. Perhaps you may want to agree with them that your grandchildren will have separate contact with you in addition to the contact they have with their non-resident parent. Remember to discuss everything with both sets of parents so everyone is aware of your wishes. If your son or daughter go through formal divorce proceedings or mediation, ask that contact and visits with their grandparents be included in their agreement about plans for their children.

Family feud

Being the parent of an adult child is not an easy role and in some families disagreements can reach a stage when sons or daughters refuse to see their parents or allow their children to have any contact. The breakdown in communication may reach the stage where months and sometimes years without contact may make any patching up seem impossible to achieve.

If you or your family have had a huge falling out with people threatening to cut off all contact, the chances are that someone, possibly everyone, will feel hurt and upset, particularly if there are children involved.

What happened?

Once people have separated they may go over events in their minds trying to figure out what happened and how the argument escalated. The truth is, you may never know – there may have been multiple reasons including, for example, the combination of a family event (wedding/funeral) and drinking one too many glasses of champagne. Big family gatherings will frequently trigger long-buried memories of sibling rivalries, old feuds and tensions may rise to the surface.

Things may have been said in the heat of the moment which, if left to fester, may leave relationships in shatters. Friends and neighbours may be asked for opinions, days turn into weeks and no one has picked up a telephone. Every family member will maintain they were right and await apologies from others. Finally, the storm in the champagne glass bubbles over into everyday life.

Apologize?

It takes maturity to step back and look at what happened and recognize that you either said something you now regret or refrained from doing something to achieve peace. There is a history in your family that only you will be able to draw on for inspiration as to how the argument can be ended. Other people's behaviour may not change but you can take full responsibility for taking the white flag out. Demonstrate to your family that you want to create a better way to relate to others and ask their advice as to how you can work with them to achieve a family life your grandchildren will be happy to observe.

Apologies are immensely powerful and a wonderful example to your grandchildren; being the family peacemaker is the way to move forward and takes strength of character. Don't go back over what happened but rather make positive plans for the future. Be warm and kind to both relatives and their chosen partners and spend time listening to some of the most interesting people in any family – the children.

Estrangement

In some families many years have passed since family members have been in touch and for some, wondering whether they are safe, whether they have had children, and questioning whether reconciling is possible becomes more urgent as time passes. Many people think that without an address or any contact details they may have lost touch forever. Family friends may mention that a son or daughter is expecting or has had a child and the grandparent may experience a renewed interest in putting their differences behind them and seeking out their family.

Even after many years it is possible to reconnect with family and enjoy a reconciliation. The Salvation Army provides an excellent service to track down family for a modest fee. Their service will give a family member, once found, a choice as to whether to pass on their current contact details or a message.

Seeking help

Families who are in conflict between generations or within couple relationships may get to a stage when each attempt to arrange a visit to a grandchild ends in tears, tantrums or abuse. When relationships are experiencing stress, those involved may wish to turn to someone outside the family to help them to cope and decide how to gain some understanding of their options. Many grandparents who telephone the Grandparents' Association helpline say they are feeling very alone in their situation. There are people who can and will help (see Taking it further).

Friends

- For many people friends will be the first calling point in dealing with the anxieties in their lives and we may value their views and opinions.
- When it comes to family relationships we may turn to people who may want to help us but they may be tempted to gossip or wade in with what you must do.
- Some people ask their friends to act as go-betweens between them and their children – think very carefully how you might feel if their friends were to approach you. Would you not prefer your children to approach you directly?
- Take care to ensure your friends can keep a confidence and discourage those you know from getting angry at your children on your behalf.
- Your friends may help by sharing fun things with you like going to a concert or a movie together rather than talk about your problems all the time.

Advice centres and advice lines

- Advice workers and volunteers will be trained to advise their clients on the specific topics covered by their service.
- Advising people on their options, rights, responsibilities and providing relevant information gives people the resources with which to make decisions and achieve an understanding of their position.
- People answering calls for the Grandparents' Association (UK) and the AARP Grandparents Center (USA) will be trained to respond to queries concerning relationships with grandchildren.

Doctors

- Most family doctors recognize that many of their patients may have pressures on them that may damage their health.
- If you are experiencing high levels of stress and/or feeling depressed, it's important to tell your doctor and discuss how your health is being affected.

Counselling and psychotherapy

- Grandparents who visit counsellors and psychotherapists are most likely to benefit from the undivided attention of someone trained to listen and observe.

- The counsellor will provide a space to talk at length about life; will give the individuals the opportunity to gain a greater understanding of their lives; and will direct their thoughts to future decisions and actions.
- The process of getting such help can be quite challenging but for many people such help enables them to move forward feeling stronger and more in control of their lives.
- Spending time with a counsellor can help identify some of the emotional barriers getting in the way of family relationships.

Mediation

- In some families all attempts at reconciliation have been abandoned and the fear of a permanent loss of contact looms. In this situation it may be appropriate to consider using the services of a professional mediator.
- Mediators are trained and experienced in exploring with family members the possibility of moving forward in a way that all family members can agree to.
- Mediation is voluntary for all involved and can only be effective with willing participants.
- Mediation offers a 'safe space' to talk and make decisions relating to children.
- Mediators will enable people to come to a shared agreement and put it in writing.

Checklist

1 Plan your visits in advance to see your children and grandchildren.

2 Have a diary planning session every few months with your family members.

3 Consider sharing family holidays together.

4 Accept that there may be conflicting demands at key holiday times like Christmas or Thanksgiving.

5 Try to maintain contact with your grandchildren in the case of divorce or separation.

6 Provide emotional as well as practical support for your child during divorce.

7 Don't criticize the behaviour of the other person in the divorce.

8 Try and agree a schedule of visits if your family member no longer has custody of your grandchildren.

9 If you are estranged, there are services that can bring you together.

10 Ultimately the courts can make a contact order with grandparents if they feel it is in the best interests of the child.

14

grandchildren living with grandparents

In this chapter you will learn:
- what to do if you become the full-time carer for your grandchildren
- what financial help may be available
- what to do about housing and education
- how to take care of your own emotional needs.

In most families grandparents will provide a safety net for their grandchildren, caring for them on a temporary basis whilst their parents take a holiday break or perhaps whilst recovering from an illness or an operation. For some grandparents the times when the parents need substantial help becomes more and more frequent and the grandparents may become increasingly concerned for the well-being of their grandchildren. There may be problems in the parents' lives such as abuse of drugs, alcohol, domestic violence or their own mental health, which overtake their ability to provide adequate care for their children.

Full-time grandparenting

Grandparents whose adult children experience problems that threaten the happiness and welfare of their children will face the dilemma of how to support the family in a way that protects the children. Such help may initially include taking the children out of the family home to stay with grandparents to give the parents a break. It may then extend to full-time care if the parental situation does not rectify itself.

Maisy's story

Maisy lived in the same street as her son Jeff, his wife Bella and their children. While Jeff spent long hours away from home working, his wife would spend more and more of her time watching television, placing bets on sports and drinking neat gin. When she lost money gambling she would lose her temper with the children and beat them with a riding whip. Maisy dropped by every day when the children were small and took her grandchildren for a walk, she would then take them back to her house for a meal and return to tuck them up in bed when her son was back from work.

When Bella was diagnosed as having some serious mental health problems Jeff asked his mother to look after the children to enable him to continue working to support his family. The children moved in with their grandmother and although Bella often came to visit them with Jeff it was Maisy who provided the main source of care throughout their childhood.

Grandparents witnessing the struggles of their adult children may feel racked with guilt; feeling that as parents they may have failed to protect their children from the lifestyle they have chosen as adults. At times such as these it can be very helpful to contact a relevant agency for support and help to distance yourself from your child's behaviour. It can be very hard to come to terms with, for example, the manipulative behaviour which may stem from substance abuse. Your adult child's problems with drugs or alcohol are not your fault; they have an illness and will need help and support to reverse their dependence on drugs or alcohol. You cannot force them to change by threats or promises – only they can decide to seek treatment. You can help your grandchildren by being there for them and supporting their needs when their parents are unable to be a good enough parent themselves.

Some grandparents may find themselves looking after their grandchildren as a result of someone from a social work team making the decision that the children can no longer be left with their parents. This decision is only made when there is ample evidence that children will thrive in the care of grandparents when their parents are no longer able to raise them. Taking on the full-time care of one or more children is a life-changing and expensive experience and it's vital that the correct advice and help is obtained.

Grandparents and the law

Grandparents who have their grandchildren living with them will need to think carefully about finding the right legal advice. It's important that the grandparents find a legal firm with knowledge and experience of assisting grandparents to obtain appropriate legal status. Grandparents will need the recognition provided by such a status to enable them to act on behalf of their grandchildren in matters relating to schooling, health and for some financial assistance to raise their grandchild.

Important considerations

Money

In both the US and the UK grandparents may be eligible to apply for a range of financial help in the form of benefits or tax breaks. It is likely that you will need some help in finding out which benefits are best for you to apply for. The AARP Grandparenting Center (USA) and the Grandparents' Association (UK) have information and assistance to help you make a claim for financial help.

Housing

Taking on responsibility for grandchildren may put a strain on the space within your home, particularly if you have recently downsized in preparation for retirement. Some grand-families in the US may benefit from a recent movement to develop specialist housing to meet their needs but at the time of writing such schemes have not reached the UK. If you are a tenant of a housing association or local authority in the UK you will need to notify your landlord of your changed circumstances and apply to be moved to a larger place.

Education

You may need to find a new school for your grandchildren in your locality.

Once your grandchildren have enrolled, make sure that their class teacher is aware of their home situation and work with the teacher to help your grandchildren settle in. Keep in touch with the teacher, if your grandchildren have previously missed out on schooling or seem to be having difficulties ask for them to be assessed for receiving extra help.

Health

Remember to register your grandchildren with a doctor and dentist in your neighbourhood. Healthcare in the UK is free on the NHS and in the US you can receive help with the cost of healthcare through initiatives such as Children's Health Insurance Program.

Taking care of yourself and your partner

Becoming a full-time grandparent is a big challenge and in taking on your grandchildren you may feel very alone and different to other grandparents.

Don't hesitate to pick up the phone or email those who can help. There are 2.4 million grandparents raising their grandchildren in the US and 250,000 families are chosen to raise their grandchildren as an alternative to foster care or adoption in the UK. It is well worth the effort to meet up with others who are in the same family situation by joining a support group or attending conferences and seminars.

Take time out by arranging for regular help with babysitting or perhaps a part-time or full-time placement at a local daycare centre for younger children. Family members and friends may be happy to help – don't be shy about asking once your grandchildren have settled in.

Checklist

1 If you become a full-time carer of your grandchildren because of difficulties in your children's lives, don't blame yourself for their problems.

2 Seek legal advice about your rights and responsibilities if you become legally responsible for your grandchildren.

3 Make sure you take advantage of the tax breaks and financial benefits available to you as the sole carer of your grandchildren.

4 Consider your housing options carefully. You may want to postpone moving to a smaller home, and you may be eligible for help from your local authority.

5 You may need to find a new school for your grandchildren. Let the teacher know about the home situation.

6 Make sure you find a new doctor for your grandchildren.

7 Get extra help and support for yourself, such as babysitting or cleaning.

8 Join a grandparents' support group.

15
grandparents and teenagers

In this chapter you will learn:
- how to listen to teenagers
- why the teenage years are so tough
- how to resolve conflicts and problems.

Grandparents can find communicating with young adolescents from the ages of 11 years old to 19 years old a real challenge; the child is moving towards adulthood and making the first attempts at separation and independence through a fog of hormones. A trusted grandparent often plays an important part in supporting a teenager's ability to communicate.

Top tips

- Listen with an open mind.
- Put yourself in their shoes.
- Allow plenty of time for the child to talk and explain.
- Ask open questions designed to help your understanding.
- Acknowledge and validate the feelings they express.

The aim is to see the situation from your grandchild's perspective so that you can understand how they are experiencing life and what they feel about it. To do this properly means putting yourself, your experiences and judgements to one side; grandparents often try to think back to when they were that age to help them understand; but this can lead to interpreting what the child is saying to them through their own eyes. It is worth reminding yourself that everyone's experience is unique and that times have changed; teenagers face different challenges today.

Listening in order to understand your grandchild's life on a regular basis will mean that you are likely to be more aware of the small, everyday issues going on; these may seem trivial to you, but your level of awareness will tune you in to the kinds of things that concern young people. This will prepare you for taking their 'big' issues seriously that you might otherwise dismiss.

It is useful to be aware of both your own body language and that of your grandchild when talking. Try to remember the following points:

- Observe body language signals to pick a good moment for a talk.
- Observe body language signals to know when to back off for now.

- Mirror posture to build feelings of rapport.
- Give feedback on what non-verbal signals are saying.

When our grandchildren are young we listen to the problem and then we tell them what to do and why; it's quite simple. In adolescence, we want to encourage self-reliance so we need to stop 'Telling them what to do' or 'Giving them advice', when they don't want it. This is the single, most common reason why adolescents stop talking to their parents. By the time children hit 11 years old, parents and grandparents have had 11 years of practice at telling them what to do and it's hard to change overnight. Nor would it be appropriate to just stop dead; it's about fading out direct advice-giving so that when the 11 year old becomes 18 or 19 plus, they actively ask for our advice and then practise the free choice of an adult to take it or leave it. To help them reach this target we can use a problem-solving approach.

1 Define the problem.
2 Agree the child's level of responsibility to solve the problem.
3 Explore different suggestions for solving the problem.
4 Agree an action plan.

Question:

Teenagers often confide in grandparents more than parents. How can a grandparent avoid undermining the parents' authority, or convey areas of worry to the parents, without betraying the teenager's confidence?

Answer:

Encourage your grandchild to go to their parents themselves and if they do not want to then you could put forward an offer of speaking to their parents for them. Tell your grandchild that you are not comfortable keeping important information from your son or daughter but you will respect their decision as to whether the parent can be told. You could also offer to be with them when they tell the parents.

Look back

The teenage years are a very challenging time and when grandparents look back at their own teenage experience most will recall some good times but also some pretty awful experiences. Whatever the generation, most people will have fumbled their way through this period of life lurching between depression and anarchy!

Teenagers in the twenty-first century have mobile phones, emails and social networking websites which may, for some, enhance the challenges of the teenage years. As is usually the case, we take out our emotions on those closest to us, leaving grandparents and parents in the firing line for a teenage angst. Try to be as patient and supportive as possible during this torrid time.

If teenagers feel their grandparents are too busy in their own world to help them, they will give up trying to communicate.

Parents' stories

'I suddenly wondered where our son had gone. We had inherited a lodger who thought the house belonged to them but did not pay any rent or make any other contribution.'

'I spent a good deal of my time trying to look this 6' 2" young person in the eye and only recognizing him by sight. I knew that the person that he had become was one that I still loved but did not like. We are good friends now.'

Samantha's story

It's sometimes easier to focus on whether something is safe rather than whether it's something that will help children to grow. Samantha believes that if she had thought along these lines, her sons would not have learnt to drive, play rugby, become goalkeepers or do many other activities that they enjoyed which may have put them at risk. She thinks her grandchildren should be encouraged to undertake paper rounds, walk to school and boil a kettle because life is full of risk and it's important for young people to experience them during their formative years.

Why the teenage years are tough

When we think about being a teenager remember that they are:

- adjusting to a changing body
- coping with fluctuating emotions
- needing to become independent from parents – hence we see them hanging around together in a park or near the shops
- learning how to make relationships
- having to face exams and job decisions.

Inner pressures

- Feeling unattractive. Most teenagers will have an inferiority complex about something, whether it be their acne, their popularity, their weight, their intelligence, etc.
- Confusion stemming from a lack of advice. Most teenagers ask friends for advice but when they themselves don't know the answers how can we expect their friends to be able to give them the right advice?
- Low self-esteem that can lead to aggressive behaviour. The old saying 'We always hurt the ones we love' is so true and a teenager's frustration is often directed towards parents and grandparents. (Even though they know deep down that we love them and we will ultimately forgive them.)

Outside pressures

- Having to grow up too fast.
- Pressures to conform i.e. become sexually active and the associated problems of sexually transmitted infections and teenage pregnancies.
- Drink, drugs etc.
- Finding employment or a college or university place.
- Peer pressure with designer labels on clothes etc.
- Big ideas and little money (their friends are always receiving more money, allowed to stay out later, go to better places etc.)
- Having to meet parental expectations.

Parental expectations, even in the most caring of homes, can lead to a strong desire to win approval. Grandparents should remember that all children are unique and yet many adults expect young people to follow in their own footsteps – a specific school, university or profession. Remember that a grandchild will only have one-quarter of your genes at best so why should they be the image of you or, indeed, their parent? Don't expect them to learn by your mistakes either. You have learnt and become the person that you are by making those mistakes! Sometimes the hardest thing that we can do is stand by and let them fall, pick them up, dust them down and help them get through it. This is true all through life, particularly in terms of relationships. Failing to meet parents' expectations has been proved to lead to anorexia, bulimia etc.

John's story

John was an intelligent young man who, despite all attempts by his parents, grandparents and teachers, rarely handed in his coursework or obtained the marks that were expected of him. When he did hand work in it never reached the A grades expected of him. His family and teachers put help on offer and become angry and frustrated with what they saw as his laziness. John began to sink into a depression; he refused to go to school, curling up in a tight ball in his bed.

His grandmother was pleased to help his parents fund the cost of educational testing when her daughter began to wonder if there were other problems apart from his depression. The educational psychologist tested John and identified that he had a specific learning difficulty which meant he had difficulty combining information from multiple sources that was particularly relevant to his ability to do coursework.

John was very relieved to gain an understanding of his problems and he was supported to understand that help would be available to him for the future. He chose to work with young children and study for his professional childcare qualifications. He hopes to work as a teacher where his understanding of a difficult adolescence will be invaluable.

Linda-Anne's story

Linda-Anne believes that encouraging children, especially boys, to cook, wash-up, do the clothes washing and ironing etc. is vital. She always believed that her sons should live with a partner through love and not because they were unable to look after themselves. Now she is a grandmother she hopes that their partners agree that she achieved this. Her sons take a big part in raising her grandchildren.

Problems and conflict

Never think that experiencing conflict with your teenager is unusual. Grandparents who have full-time care of their grandchild may take this opportunity to feel some sort of guilt at this stage, particularly if the trauma that brought the grandchild to them involved behaviour by their own child that the grandparent found unacceptable or unable to cope with (i.e. drug abuse or mental health issues). This is certainly not the time for anyone within the family to mutter those immortal lines 'You're turning into your father/mother'. This will set off a fear within the young person themselves and will not improve any relationship.

Conflict may be a necessity for some children to assert their independence. All children want to establish themselves as individuals. This is true whether they have siblings or when they grow up and want to show that they are not a mini version of their parents.

Whose problem?

There are at least two sides to problems within families. Who really has the problem? Who is really upset about it? It could be you, the child or both of you.

Here are some tips in handling a teenager's problem:

- Listen to them without other distractions or interruptions.
- Acknowledge their feelings and empathize.
- Don't give them advice unless they ask for it.
- Don't take the problem on yourself.
- Talk about what the cause of the problem may be.
- Discuss what might help them to solve the problem.
- Think through the consequences.

If it is more of an adult problem, try to have a united front (at least in public) with your spouse or partner and the parents. Try to share a firm but friendly approach to adolescent behaviour.

Ultimately, try to avoid conflict. Conflict in relationships between adults and teenagers usually results in anger. Think about how you feel when you are angry: humiliated, weepy, furious, revengeful etc., so why do we expect the teenager not to have the same feelings? Conflict can rarely be resolved if both sides are experiencing the same negative feelings. The old wartime saying of 'Jaw jaw is better than war war' still holds true.

Making it worse

You have a choice as to how you deal with conflict. It can become worse if you:

- Meet it head on – needing to control or win whatever situation is put in front of you either leads to forced submission or outright rebellion.
- Avoid conflict at any cost – giving in to have a quiet life always ends up in resentment, as people may feel used and the problems are not resolved.
- Seethe silently – sulking and the answer that 'nothing's wrong' leads to an unpleasant atmosphere for everyone.

Making it better

The alternative way forward is to:

- Be open, honest and agree that both of you have the right to say how you feel.
- Don't try talking when the television is on or there are other people around – really listening requires a lot of attention and thought.
- When you have heard the views of the parent or grandchild, check that you have understood.

- Try giving a choice, negotiation or compromise and then make a decision.
- Monitor the result of this decision.
- If you can move some way towards centre ground it will at least give the young person the knowledge that you have listened and are ready to hear their side of the story.
- Who knows, your family may come to you in the future before a situation has reached crisis point.

Rosemary's story

There may be some situations where ignoring some of the issues can produce the best outcomes. My grandson's permanently untidy room drove me to distraction but he said that he needed his privacy. We reached a form of compromise. He would keep the door closed, clean his own room, bring plates, cups etc. downstairs and do his own washing and ironing. It was not ideal but he got his privacy and it stopped the almost daily conflict. A small price to pay!

Remember that the teenage years are likely to be more difficult and confusing for the young person in your family than they are for you. Encourage and praise every step in the right direction. Take a lot of interest in their work and ask lots of questions. Value their contribution to family life and share a confidence that they will be able to find their way through the confusion.

Checklist

1 Try and see things from your grandchild's perspective.

2 Keep in touch by listening carefully on a regular basis without distractions.

3 Observe body language signals to decide when is a good moment to communicate or back off, and give feedback on what you think the non verbal-signals are saying.

4 Don't give advice unless they ask for it.

5 Help them define their problems and explore possible solutions.

6 Remember your own experiences as a teenager to keep things in perspective.

7 Acknowledge their feelings and show empathy.

8 Try and negotiate a solution rather than get into a head-on conflict.

9 Keep a united front between grandparents and parents.

appendix 1

How to use Skype

Skype is a popular program for people to stay in touch across the world. It is one of a number of different programs that use the internet to make calls to other computers. What you must have to get started is an internet connection, and a computer (Mac or PC – either is fine) which is equipped with speakers and a microphone. It is very easy for everyone to use, and it allows you to keep in touch in three useful ways:

1 You can make telephone calls for free to other computers who also have the Skype program.
2 You can use Skype to call normal telephone numbers – mobile or landline – anywhere in the world. For this you have to add credit to your Skype account by using a credit or debit card and paying online. Often the rates are cheaper than a regular telephone call.
3 You can use Skype to have a video chat. For this, you and the person you are chatting with must both be using a webcam – a camera which plugs into your computer and records video. For video chat, it is best if you also have a fast broadband internet connection.

To use Skype, you must download the Skype program from the company's website: www.skype.com. Once you are on this website, follow the links to download the program to save it onto your computer. As with other programs that you download from the internet, save the program file (it will be called SkypeSetup.exe, or something similar) onto your computer first. This may take a while as the file is large – around 20 megabytes. Once the download is finished, you must use the file you have downloaded to install the program.

Open the file which you just saved (you may have to click 'Run' if you are asked whether you want to install it) and follow the instructions on the screen to install Skype on your computer.

After Skype has been successfully installed, you will need to create a Skype account in order to use the program. This is very easy. A screen will pop up the first time you use Skype that asks you to provide some personal details. At a minimum, you just need to create a user name for the account (e.g. 'Joe Bloggs' or 'Grandad 1944'), set a password for your new Skype account, and provide Skype with your valid email address so that they can contact you.

Once you are set up with an account and the program is open and running you will be 'online'. At any given time, there may be up to 10 million other Skype users online too – perhaps friends and relatives but plenty of people you have never met. Other people will be able to find you by searching for your user name or your email address, and you will be able to find them. However, if you want to, you can set Skype so that you are 'invisible' to all other Skype users by clicking on the green tick in the bottom left of the Skype window. To find someone to call, click on Tools (at the top of the Skype window) and then select 'Search for Skype users' on the drop down menu that appears. Follow the instructions to search for the person you are looking for. Once you find them, you simply double click on their name to start a call. Every person you successfully find will appear in your list of Contacts in the Skype window.

The Skype website has plenty of helpful advice including how to send a text message using Skype, how to start a video chat if you have a webcam, or how to use Skype and your credit or debit card to pay for cheap telephone calls to normal phone lines. Go to www.skype.com/help/guides to read more about the many features of the program.

appendix 2

Playdough recipes to make at home

Regular playdough

Ingredients

2 cups plain flour
1 cup salt
2 cups cold water
2 tbsp vegetable oil
4 tsp cream of tartar

Optional: few drops food colouring and/or glitter

Method

Mix the flour, salt and cream of tartar (also the glitter, if using) together in a saucepan. Gradually add the cold water, vegetable oil and food colouring. Cook the playdough on a low heat, stirring all the time until the mixture slowly thickens into a big stretchy elastic mass that is so stiff you can't stir it anymore. Tip out the dough onto a work surface and wait a few moments until you are sure it is cool enough for you to handle. Knead for a few minutes until you get a smooth, soft and pliable dough.

Your playdough is now ready to use.

Store in an airtight container in the refrigerator and it should keep for a couple of weeks at least.

Microwave playdough

Ingredients
2 cups plain flour
2 cups salt
2 cups cold water
2 tbsp oil
4 tsp cream of tartar
Food colouring

Method
Mix all ingredients together in large bowl. Cook in microwave for one minute on high power. Remove and stir well. Cook in microwave for one minute more. Knead well.

No cook modelling dough

Ingredients
1 lb plain flour
1 lb salt
Cold water, as required

Method
Simply mix the flour and salt together with cold water to make a dough.

This is great for rolling out to cut out shapes, and modeling all sorts of pretend food, decorations and animals!

Useful organizations in the UK

Adoption UK
Tel: 01795 661463
Website: www.adoptionuk.org.uk
Information and support for adoptive families and potential adopters.

Al Anon
Tel: 020 7403 0888
Website: www.al-anonuk.org.uk
Al Anon provides understanding, strength and hope to those whose lives are affected by someone else's drinking.

Bilingualism
Website: www.bilingualism.co.uk

BLISS The premature baby charity
Tel: 0500 618140
Website: www.bliss.org.uk
Helpline for parents and relatives of sick or premature babies.

Breastfeeding line
Tel: 0870 444 8708
Website: www.nctpregnancyandbabycare.com
Helpline on breastfeeding for mothers, pregnant women and their families.

Child Death Helpline

Tel: 0800 282986

Website: www.childdeathline.org.uk

Helpline for those grieving the loss of a child of any age, however recently or long ago.

Childline Helpline

Tel: 0800 1111

Website: www.childline.org.uk

Help for children and young people in distress, designed for children to access help for themselves in times of distress.

Childminding Helpline

Tel: 0800 169 4486

Website: www.ncma.org.uk

A resource both for families seeking a childminder and grandparents who wish to become childminders in the UK.

Child Protection Helpline NSPCC

Tel: 0808 800 5000

Website: www.nspcc.org.uk

Counselling, information and advice to anyone concerned about a child at risk of abuse. Staffed by social workers experienced in child protection.

Children's Information Service

Tel: 0800 096 0206

Website: www.childcarelink.gov.uk

All local authorities now hold information on the services and facilities that childcare providers in their local area can offer. To find your local service check out the website.

Compassionate Friends

Tel: 0845 123 2304

Helpline for families experiencing the loss of their son or daughter at any stage of their lives.

Criminal Records Bureau (CRB)

Tel: 0870 9090 811

Website: www.crb.gov.uk

The role of the CRB is to reduce risk of child abuse by helping to identify those unsuitable to work with children. Gives information on how to apply for or obtain a CRB check.

Cry-sis
Tel: 08451 228 669
Website: www.cry-sis.org.uk
Helpline for families of babies who are crying, sleepless and/or very demanding. Offer suggestions for calming babies and a listening supportive response but not medical advice.

Contact a Family
Tel: 0808 808 3555
Website: www.cafamily.org.uk
Helpline and advice for family members who care for children with disabilities or special needs. Contact a Family can direct you to organizations that assist with specific disabilities, including rare conditions, and self help groups.

Drugs Helpline
Tel: 0800 7766600
Website: www.talktofrank.com
National service providing confidential advice and information for anyone looking for support relating to drug use.

Domestic Violence Refuge
Tel : 0808 200 0247
Website: www.refuge.org.uk
Staffed by women – a 24-hour service for people experiencing domestic violence.

Education – Advisory Centre for Education
Tel: 0808 800 5793
Website: www.ace-ed.org.uk
Advice line providing information and advice on state funded education for children 5–16 years old.

Education – OFSTED
Website: www.ofsted.gov.uk
The new OFSTED now publishes reports on all state schools and also on childcare providers including nurseries and childminders. All reports can be downloaded from their website.

Education Otherwise
Website: www.education-otherwise.org
Provides support and information to families whose children are being educated outside school.

Families need Fathers
Tel: 08707 607 496
Website: www.fnf.org.uk
Support, advice and information on children's issues for separated and divorced parents. Works with family members to ensure children retain access to both parents and their wider families.

Families Anonymous
Tel: 0845 120 0660
Website: www.famanon.org.uk
Telephone and other support services for families and friends of people who may have a problem with substance abuse.

Grandparents' Association
Moot House,
The Stow,
Harlow, Essex CM20 3AG
Advice line: 0845 434 9585
Tel: 0845 4349585
Website: www.grandparents-association.org.uk

The national membership organization for grandparents in the UK provides:
• support for grandparents who have lost or are losing contact with their grandchildren
• support for those caring for their grandchildren on a full time basis
• support for grandparents who have childcare responsibilities for their grandchildren
• welfare benefits advice
• grandparent and toddler groups
• lists of family solicitors.

I CAN
Website: www.ican.org.uk
8 Wakley Street,
London
EC1V 7QE

I CAN is the children's communication charity. It runs schools and services to support children's communication and has resources and advice for families.

Mediation – National Family Mediation
7 The Close,
Exeter,
Devon,
EX1 1EZ
Tel: 01392 271610
Website: www.nfm.org.uk

National Family Mediation can put you in touch with your nearest mediation service. The service will have an initial meeting with you to discuss the process of mediation, their charges and whether it will be appropriate for your situation.

National Childbirth Trust
The National Childbirth Trust (NCT) is the largest and best-known childbirth and parenting charity in Europe. It is the voice of parents on antenatal, birth and postnatal issues, and provides a range of quality educational and support services for parents at local level. Established 50 years ago, the NCT has successfully campaigned for improved care during pregnancy and childbirth and promotes the principle of informed choice for women and their partners.

NCT provides a range of services for any new parents including antenatal classes, postnatal discussion groups, breastfeeding counselling and a network of local groups in the UK.

Pre School Learning Alliance
Tel: 020 7697 2500
Website: www.pre-school.org.uk

The Pre School Learning Alliance is a leading educational charity specializing in the early years. They provide back up support to over 15,000 groups providing support for under fives, and their staff and volunteers contribute to the care and education of over 800,000 young children and their families each year. The PSLA support and actively promote family involvement in all aspects of their work.

Relate
Tel: 0845 456 131
Website: www.relate.org.uk

Relate offers advice, relationship counselling, sex therapy, workshops, mediation, consultations and support to couples, families and individuals.

Salvation Army Family Tracing Service
Tel: 0845 634 4747
Website: www.salvationarmy.org.uk
A service for families to reconnect to relatives.

Samaritans
Tel: 0845 90 90 90
Website: www.samaritans.org.uk
National helpline offering emotional support for people who are feeling distress or despair, including those situations which may lead to suicide.

Books

Miscarriage: what every woman needs to know, Lesley Regan (2001), Bloomsbury.

Babyshock!, Elizabeth Martyn and Relate (2001), Vermillion

The Secret of Happy Parents, Steve Biddulph (2004), Thorsons.

Successful Potty Training, Heather Welford (2002), National Childbirth Trust Guides.

Raising Happy Children, Jan Parker and Jan Stimpson (2004), Hodder and Stoughton Ltd.

What Every Parent Needs to Know. The Incredible Effects of Love, Nurture and Play on your Child's Development, Margot Sunderland (2007), Dorling Kindersley.

Related by Adoption: A Handbook for Grandparents and Other Relatives, British Association of Adoption and Fostering (2004).

How to Survive and Thrive in an Empty Nest, J & R Lauer (1999), New Harbinger Publications.

The Good Toy Guide, Toy Library Association.

5-minute First Aid for Babies, The British Red Cross (2005), Hodder Arnold.

5-minute First Aid for Children, The British Red Cross (2005), Hodder Arnold.

Adolescence: The Survival Guide for Parents and Teenagers, Elizabeth Fenwick and Dr Tony Smith (1998), Dorling Kindersley.

Stop Arguing: Start Talking, Susan Quilliam and Relate (2001), Vermillion.

The Real Meaning of Money, Dorothy Rowe (1998), Harper Collins.

Help Your Children Cope with Your Divorce, Relate (2007).

Mum and Dad Split Up, Elizabeth O'Loughlin and Kayleigh Adams, Pangolin Books (2005).

(A children's book which tells the story of a family splitting up through the eyes of their young child. Provides support for children by acknowledging the distress that parental separation causes to a young child and by emphasizing the importance of their talking to others about how they are feeling. It is aimed at children aged 5 years and over.)

My Parents are Getting Divorced: How to Keep it Together When Your Mom and Dad are Splitting Up, Florence Cadier, Melissa Daly and Claire Gandini, (2004) Harry N. Abrams Inc.

(A book for older children which aims to answer some of the questions they might have when their parents decide to separate or divorce. Aims to help children cope with new situations and changes within the family. Includes a list of resources.)

Factsheets

(Available free of charge from the Grandparents' Association – www.grandparents-association.org.uk)

- Guardians
- The Children's Guardian
- The Reporting Officer
- Residence Orders
- Contact with a grandchild looked after by a local authority
- Contact with a grandchild
- Adoption
- Parental Responsibility
- Contact arguments
- Drug abuse and the care of children.

Other books also available from the Grandparents' Association include:

- *Looking after Your Grandchild* (ISBN 0952026732)
- *Jettison the Jargon* (ISBN 0952026740)
- *Relative Values – Best Interests of the Child* (ISBN 0952026767)

- *An Evaluation of Grandparent and Toddler Groups* (ISBN 0952026778)
- *The Children Act – What's in it for Grandparents?* (ISBN 0952026792)
- *Being a Grandparent: Research Evidence and Key Themes* (ISBN 0952026785)
- The latest magazine of the Grandparents' Association, *Grandparent Times*.

Other resources

The National Association of Toy and Leisure Libraries can give details of local community resources to support children's play. Their members are happy to advise grandparents and loan equipment and toys to grandparents looking after their grandchildren.

England Tel: 020 7255 4616
Scotland Tel: 0131 664 2746
Wales Tel: 01874 622 097
Email: www.natll.org.uk

Learning with Grandparents Pack
A series of leaflets has been produced as part of a collaborative project by the Basic Skills Agency involving grandparents, schools, Grandparents Plus and the Grandparents' Association.

The pack includes a jargon-busting guide to the everyday life of primary schools. This will tell you about mind maps, extended schools and SATS. Another resource aims to encourage correspondence with grandparents who live a distance away. 'It doesn't Take Much to Stay in Touch' includes keeping-in-touch postcards – a book of 24 delightful postcards, pre-printed with ideas to encourage written communication between grandparents and grandchildren. It comes with a 'Things to do when you are Apart' booklet with suggestions and ideas for supporting grandchildren's learning from a distance.

Published by Basic Skills Agency at NIACE.

***Chatter Matters* DVD**
Chatter Matters is a DVD which will help grandparents support their children's communication development, presented by Dr Tanya Byron. It can be ordered free of charge by families from I CAN.

Child Psychotherapy Trust Leaflets
Email: www.understandingchildhhood.net

Understanding childhood offers leaflets on children's emotional development from birth to adulthood. These informative and easy-to-read leaflets were written by experienced child and adolescent psychotherapists for the Child Psychotherapy Trust.

Useful organizations in the US

AARP Foundation Grandparent Information Center (GIC)

AARP Foundation Grandparent Information Center,
601 E Street, NW,
Washington, DC 20049
Tel: 1-888-OUR-AARP (1-888-687-2277)
Fax: 1-202-434-6466
Email: gic@aarp.org

This organization provides :

- Initiatives around work issues for grandfamilies, benefits outreach and financial literacy.
- GIC Database – a searchable, online database that connects grandparents raising grandchildren and/or those seeking visitation with local supportive services and programmes.
- GIC Website – a website with lots of articles, state factsheets, and message board.
- GIC Materials – research about grandparenting (booklets in English and some are available in Spanish as well).
- Technical assistance and networking for local, state, and national organizations.
- Benefits QuickLINK.
- Subscription to *GrandCare News* – a free quarterly newsletter for grandparents who are caring for their grandchildren and professionals who support them.

The AARP Foundation Grandparent Information Center (GIC) has a variety of resources to help grandparents in various family roles, and for the professionals who work with them.

It is part of the AARP Foundation Grandparenting Program, whose goal is to ensure that grandparents and grandchildren have access to resources that strengthen their health, finances and family connections.

It also provides information, referral and outreach for:

- grandparents providing childcare for their grandchildren
- grandparents raising grandchildren full-time
- grandparents who have problems with visiting their grandchildren
- grandparents who want to have a positive role in their grandchildren's lives.

The centre also provides information for professionals, including:

- employers, human resources professionals, employee assistance programs
- corporate professionals
- teachers and school administrators
- healthcare professionals
- advocates and policy makers
- other service providers.

Apples 4 the teacher
www.apples4theteacher.com
Free, educational website: fun for kids covering maths, literacy, science and art.

Casey Family Programs
www.casey.org
Casey works in partnership with local city communities to create stable family support for children.

Center for Understanding Aging
P.O. Box 246
Southington, CT 06489
(860) 621-2079

Center on Schools, Families and Community Partnership
3003 North Charles Street
Baltimore, MD 21218
(410) 516-8800

Children's Defense Fund (CDF)
www.childrensdefense.org
25 East Street, N.W.
Washington, D.C. 20001
(202) 628-8787
CDF advocate on behalf of children in the areas of child development, health, mental health and family income.

Community Update
US Department of Education
Washington, D.C. 20202-0498
1-USA-LEARN

Child Welfare League of America
www.cwla.org
Resources and best practice guidance on grandparents and other relatives raising children in the foster care system. Information on child protection and state child welfare agencies.

Generations United
www.grandsplace.org
Factsheets about grandparents and other relatives raising grandchildren.

Grandsplace
Legal resources, chat room for grandparent caregivers.

Grand Parent Again
www.grandparentagain.com
Support and guidance for grandparents raising their own children.

KINship Information Network
Informational and emotional support for grandparents and other relatives raising children.

National Committee of Grandparents for Children's Rights
Advocates and lobbies for legislative changes to support grandparents.

The Brookdale Foundation Group
www.brookdalefoundation.org
National network of support groups for grandparents and other relatives raising children and mini-grant program for new groups

The Family Involvement Partnership for Learning
600 Independence Avenue, SW
Washington, D.C. 20202-8173
(800) USA-LEARN

The Foundation for Grandparenting
www.grandparenting.org
A non-profit organization dedicated to supporting grandparents.

teach yourself ®

From Advanced Sudoku to Zulu, you'll find everything you need in the **teach yourself** range, in books, on CD and on DVD.

Visit **www.teachyourself.co.uk** for more details.

Advanced Sudoku and Kakuro
Afrikaans
Alexander Technique
Algebra
Ancient Greek
Applied Psychology
Arabic
Arabic Conversation
Aromatherapy
Art History
Astrology
Astronomy
AutoCAD 2004
AutoCAD 2007
Ayurveda
Baby Massage and Yoga
Baby Signing
Baby Sleep
Bach Flower Remedies
Backgammon
Ballroom Dancing
Basic Accounting
Basic Computer Skills
Basic Mathematics
Beauty
Beekeeping
Beginner's Arabic Script
Beginner's Chinese Script
Beginner's Dutch

Beginner's French
Beginner's German
Beginner's Greek
Beginner's Greek Script
Beginner's Hindi
Beginner's Hindi Script
Beginner's Italian
Beginner's Japanese
Beginner's Japanese Script
Beginner's Latin
Beginner's Mandarin Chinese
Beginner's Portuguese
Beginner's Russian
Beginner's Russian Script
Beginner's Spanish
Beginner's Turkish
Beginner's Urdu Script
Bengali
Better Bridge
Better Chess
Better Driving
Better Handwriting
Biblical Hebrew
Biology
Birdwatching
Blogging
Body Language
Book Keeping
Brazilian Portuguese

Bridge
British Citizenship Test, The
British Empire, The
British Monarchy from Henry
  VIII, The
Buddhism
Bulgarian
Bulgarian Conversation
Business French
Business Plans
Business Spanish
Business Studies
C++
Calculus
Calligraphy
Cantonese
Caravanning
Car Buying and Maintenance
Card Games
Catalan
Chess
Chi Kung
Chinese Medicine
Christianity
Classical Music
Coaching
Cold War, The
Collecting
Computing for the Over 50s
Consulting
Copywriting
Correct English
Counselling
Creative Writing
Cricket
Croatian
Crystal Healing
CVs
Czech
Danish
Decluttering
Desktop Publishing
Detox
Digital Home Movie Making
Digital Photography
Dog Training
Drawing

Dream Interpretation
Dutch
Dutch Conversation
Dutch Dictionary
Dutch Grammar
Eastern Philosophy
Electronics
English as a Foreign Language
English Grammar
English Grammar as a Foreign
  Language
Entrepreneurship
Estonian
Ethics
Excel 2003
Feng Shui
Film Making
Film Studies
Finance for Non-Financial
  Managers
Finnish
First World War, The
Fitness
Flash 8
Flash MX
Flexible Working
Flirting
Flower Arranging
Franchising
French
French Conversation
French Dictionary
French for Homebuyers
French Grammar
French Phrasebook
French Starter Kit
French Verbs
French Vocabulary
Freud
Gaelic
Gaelic Conversation
Gaelic Dictionary
Gardening
Genetics
Geology
German
German Conversation

German Grammar
German Phrasebook
German Starter Kit
German Vocabulary
Globalization
Go
Golf
Good Study Skills
Great Sex
Green Parenting
Greek
Greek Conversation
Greek Phrasebook
Growing Your Business
Guitar
Gulf Arabic
Hand Reflexology
Hausa
Herbal Medicine
Hieroglyphics
Hindi
Hindi Conversation
Hinduism
History of Ireland, The
Home PC Maintenance and
  Networking
How to DJ
How to Run a Marathon
How to Win at Casino Games
How to Win at Horse Racing
How to Win at Online Gambling
How to Win at Poker
How to Write a Blockbuster
Human Anatomy & Physiology
Hungarian
Icelandic
Improve Your French
Improve Your German
Improve Your Italian
Improve Your Spanish
Improving Your Employability
Indian Head Massage
Indonesian
Instant French
Instant German
Instant Greek
Instant Italian

Instant Japanese
Instant Portuguese
Instant Russian
Instant Spanish
Internet, The
Irish
Irish Conversation
Irish Grammar
Islam
Israeli-Palestinian Conflict, The
Italian
Italian Conversation
Italian for Homebuyers
Italian Grammar
Italian Phrasebook
Italian Starter Kit
Italian Verbs
Italian Vocabulary
Japanese
Japanese Conversation
Java
JavaScript
Jazz
Jewellery Making
Judaism
Jung
Kama Sutra, The
Keeping Aquarium Fish
Keeping Pigs
Keeping Poultry
Keeping a Rabbit
Knitting
Korean
Latin
Latin American Spanish
Latin Dictionary
Latin Grammar
Letter Writing Skills
Life at 50: For Men
Life at 50: For Women
Life Coaching
Linguistics
LINUX
Lithuanian
Magic
Mahjong
Malay

Managing Stress
Managing Your Own Career
Mandarin Chinese
Mandarin Chinese Conversation
Marketing
Marx
Massage
Mathematics
Meditation
Middle East Since 1945, The
Modern China
Modern Hebrew
Modern Persian
Mosaics
Music Theory
Mussolini's Italy
Nazi Germany
Negotiating
Nepali
New Testament Greek
NLP
Norwegian
Norwegian Conversation
Old English
One-Day French
One-Day French – the DVD
One-Day German
One-Day Greek
One-Day Italian
One-Day Polish
One-Day Portuguese
One-Day Spanish
One-Day Spanish – the DVD
One-Day Turkish
Origami
Owning a Cat
Owning a Horse
Panjabi
PC Networking for Small
  Businesses
Personal Safety and Self
  Defence
Philosophy
Philosophy of Mind
Philosophy of Religion
Phone French
Phone German

Phone Italian
Phone Japanese
Phone Mandarin Chinese
Phone Spanish
Photography
Photoshop
PHP with MySQL
Physics
Piano
Pilates
Planning Your Wedding
Polish
Polish Conversation
Politics
Portuguese
Portuguese Conversation
Portuguese for Homebuyers
Portuguese Grammar
Portuguese Phrasebook
Postmodernism
Pottery
PowerPoint 2003
PR
Project Management
Psychology
Quick Fix French Grammar
Quick Fix German Grammar
Quick Fix Italian Grammar
Quick Fix Spanish Grammar
Quick Fix: Access 2002
Quick Fix: Excel 2000
Quick Fix: Excel 2002
Quick Fix: HTML
Quick Fix: Windows XP
Quick Fix: Word
Quilting
Recruitment
Reflexology
Reiki
Relaxation
Retaining Staff
Romanian
Running Your Own Business
Russian
Russian Conversation
Russian Grammar
Sage Line 50

Sanskrit
Screenwriting
Second World War, The
Serbian
Setting Up a Small Business
Shorthand Pitman 2000
Sikhism
Singing
Slovene
Small Business Accounting
Small Business Health Check
Songwriting
Spanish
Spanish Conversation
Spanish Dictionary
Spanish for Homebuyers
Spanish Grammar
Spanish Phrasebook
Spanish Starter Kit
Spanish Verbs
Spanish Vocabulary
Speaking On Special Occasions
Speed Reading
Stalin's Russia
Stand Up Comedy
Statistics
Stop Smoking
Sudoku
Swahili
Swahili Dictionary
Swedish
Swedish Conversation
Tagalog
Tai Chi
Tantric Sex
Tap Dancing
Teaching English as a Foreign
    Language
Teams & Team Working
Thai
Thai Conversation
Theatre
Time Management
Tracing Your Family History
Training
Travel Writing
Trigonometry

Turkish
Turkish Conversation
Twentieth Century USA
Typing
Ukrainian
Understanding Tax for Small
    Businesses
Understanding Terrorism
Urdu
Vietnamese
Visual Basic
Volcanoes, Earthquakes and
    Tsunamis
Watercolour Painting
Weight Control through Diet &
    Exercise
Welsh
Welsh Conversation
Welsh Dictionary
Welsh Grammar
Wills & Probate
Windows XP
Wine Tasting
Winning at Job Interviews
Word 2003
World Faiths
Writing Crime Fiction
Writing for Children
Writing for Magazines
Writing a Novel
Writing a Play
Writing Poetry
Xhosa
Yiddish
Yoga
Your Wedding
Zen
Zulu